My Life and the Final Days of Hollywood

Claude Jarman Jr.

ISBN 978-1-64003-667-3 (Paperback)
ISBN 978-1-64003-668-0 (Digital)

Covenant Books, Inc.
11661 Hwy 707
Murrells Inlet, SC 29576
www.covenantbooks.com

INTRODUCTION

Hollywood no longer exists. The plot of land is still there—a four-mile-square neighborhood bordered by the foothills to the north and the Spanish mansions of Hancock Park to the south, commonly referred to as Hollywood. It is not officially a city; the postmark on a letter sent from Hollywood now bears the general stamp of Los Angeles. Today this area remains a tourist destination, though there is little to see. A few blocks of movie-themed souvenir shops, an outdoor shopping mall, plenty of Starbucks, and endless lots of concrete slabs supporting seas of parked cars wedged bumper-to-chrome.

A few functioning movie studios still stand in the area. One of them provides tours in which a guide points to locations where films used to be shot, with the tacked-on explanation that the studio now rents its space to production companies shooting television series and that only one feature film every two or three years is made there. Most of the studio's revenue comes from the sale of T-shirts, key chains, and plush toys. Though strictly enforced laws prohibit the shooting of movies or TV shows on the streets of Hollywood without a costly permit, you can still spot young filmmakers staging scenes for their digital cameras on street corners around town, ready to hastily pack their gear and retreat at the first glimpse of a police car.

Though fewer and fewer films are made there, the term "Hollywood" is still bandied about in the media. Type the words "Hollywood news" into your Internet search bar and thousands of pages will result—stories and headlines that have nothing to do with the plot of land known as Hollywood, but the state of mind, the abstract designation that conjures up the American filmmaking industry, the culture of celebrity worship, and the glitz of the Oscars.

But the real Hollywood is only a memory. A memory of mythic proportions, perhaps, yet one that is very real to me and quite vivid in my mind. I was there. I lived in its final days before the swift decline, when the power and the glory that was the Hollywood studio system was at its zenith.

Early in 1945, Metro-Goldwyn-Mayer began preproduction on the screen version of Marjorie Kinnan Rawlings's Pulitzer Prize–winning novel *The Yearling*. A touching human drama set in the late 1800s, *The Yearling* told the story of a poor Floridian family, a young boy, and his pet fawn. More than twelve thousand young hopefuls from the Southern states alone auditioned for the lead role of Jody, and another seven thousand from the rest of the country. A total of over nineteen thousand boys tried for the part. One was eventually selected. I was that boy.

Whisked from the slow Southern city of Nashville, Tennessee, to the bustling epicenter of Hollywood, California, at age ten, I was the envy of kids everywhere. Gregory Peck played my father, Jane Wyman my mother, and legendary director Clarence Brown became my mentor and friend. The world I had known was shaken upside down as I left school, my friends, and Nashville to spend over one solid year of my life working on *The Yearling*. My performance earned critical acclaim and a special Academy Award, and I went on to make ten other features before leaving the movie industry.

It was quite a ride while it lasted. Formidable columnist Hedda Hopper hailed me as "filmdom's child discovery of the year" before *The Yearling* was even released. Once it debuted, I was praised by the critics and cast in a string of films opposite the likes of Van Johnson, Randolph Scott, Gloria Grahame, Donna Reed, and John Wayne. I even shot and killed Lee Marvin (on-screen, of course) in one of his first movies. Louella Parsons informed the readers of her nationwide column that child superstar Margaret O'Brien had fallen in love with me, but I only had eyes for Gregory Peck's wife. I was the closest thing to the fabled "overnight star" of Hollywood lore, and I soaked it all up. For a little while.

When I was dropped into the dream factory in the mid-1940s, the world was still at war. There was no TV, no home video, and the Internet was only a distant dream. For entertainment, people went to the movies; it was the national pastime. With no competition from war-torn Europe, Hollywood movie studios took over the world, reaping enormous profits and wielding enormous clout.

During that time, no movie studio better represented the art, business, and state of mind known as Hollywood than Metro-Goldwyn-Mayer. There were six other major studios: Paramount, Warner Bros., Columbia, RKO, Universal, and Twentieth Century Fox. But MGM was the cream of the crop. Helmed by powerful visionary and mogul Louis B. Mayer, MGM became so synonymous with Hollywood that each of its films proudly (and falsely) proclaimed "Made in Hollywood, USA" on the credits, though the MGM studio was located outside of Hollywood in nearby Culver City.

MGM was known as the studio of the stars, boasting a roster of "more stars than there are in heaven." Clark Gable, Greta Garbo, James Stewart, Judy Garland, Spencer Tracy, Katharine Hepburn, Lana Turner, Fred Astaire, Gene Kelly, Frank Sinatra, and Elizabeth Taylor were just a handful of the celluloid heroes under contract to MGM in the 1940s. Their era is the stuff of legend, but it was my reality. My name was on the roster along with them.

with Gene Kelly in 1947   with Jimmy Durante in 1945

I had lunch in the commissary every day with these luminaries. As I spooned gravy over my mashed potatoes, Katharine Hepburn would stroll by—in costume for her role as Clara Schumann in *Song of Love*—and place a napkin over her elegant 19th-century gown before sitting down to eat her meal. On any given day, Fred Astaire might dash in for lunch in a tuxedo, Gene Kelly would be costumed as a pirate, Esther Williams as a female toreador. It was a fairytale come to life.

But nothing lasts forever. By the early 1950s, television was posing a real threat to film production, and the studio system started to decline. When that happened, the fairytale was shattered. For me, it was already beginning to crumble; I was suffering from anxiety and disillusionment and nurturing a growing suspicion that there was a dark side beneath the dream factory's shimmering facade. The glamour wore off quickly for me. It took me years to be able to fully appreciate those films I made in the 1940s and '50s.

The old Metro-Goldwyn-Mayer lot was eventually taken over by Sony, a major entertainment conglomerate—whatever that means. The studio responsible for *The Wizard of Oz* now produces a wide array of content for online streaming, videogames, and cell phone apps.

When I was there in the late '40s, I remember every soundstage bustling with life and activity daily. Today, many stages sit vacant. Sony does pay homage to its illustrious roots now and then: one building is named Heidelberg (after Ernst Lubitsch's 1927 silent classic *The Student Prince in Old Heidelberg)*; a little-used office features a framed still of Jean Harlow and Robert Taylor. I wonder how many of the young people working on the Sony lot know who Harlow was. Or Lubitsch. They were even before *my* time.

MGM 25th Anniversary photo

A clip that still circulates online is footage from the famous MGM twenty-fifth anniversary luncheon in April 1949. The camera pans across the banquet tables as Ava Gardner laughs at one of Clark Gable's jokes, Greer Garson smiles at Errol Flynn, Fred Astaire shares a private joke with Judy Garland. Jimmy Durante, Lionel and Ethel Barrymore, Spencer Tracy . . . all the cinema legends are present, even Lassie. And there I am, a lanky fourteen-year-old sitting right next to Buster Keaton. When I watch that footage today, I am struck by the realization that Angela Lansbury, Dean Stockwell, Arlene Dahl, Jane Powell, and I are the only ones still living. From the Golden Age of Hollywood, I am virtually the last man standing. This is my story.

CHAPTER 1

Movies and Make Believe

In the early 1900s, Nashville, Tennessee, was a sleepy town with fewer than 100,000 residents. It had yet to find fame as Music City, USA, and the home of the Grand Ole Opry, and was known as a fairly prosperous shipping borough. Situated in the middle of the state, Nashville is the capitol and the seat of the old Nashville & Chattanooga Railroad (later known as the Nashville, Chattanooga, & St. Louis or NC&StL). To its west stands Memphis, some 220 miles away. To the east is Knoxville, a distance of 180 miles.

Fifty miles south of Nashville lies the tiny trading-post town of Fosterville. It was in this community that my father, Claude Miller Jarman, was born on March 29, 1904. He was the last of thirteen children; his twin sister, Maude, preceded him by minutes. Life was rugged, money was scarce, and pleasures were simple. The favorite pastime of Fosterville's younger residents was climbing to the top of Old Soap Stone Hill and watching the trains wind through the hills on their way to nearby Bell Buckle, Tennessee, about eight miles away. There were few jobs to be had except working for the railroad. Two of my father's brothers were engineers with the NC&StL.

When my father was twelve, both of his parents died of heart attacks and his older brother John took him in. John's wife, Sarah, resented Claude's presence in the household. To attend high school, Claude would have to ride the train to Murfreesboro, a thirty-minute trip each way. After taking her husband to the station, Sarah would return home without waiting for Claude—who was getting off the train around the same time—forcing him to walk a distance of over a mile. Like his resilient pioneer ancestors, my father persevered through the adversity. He graduated from high school and landed a job at a bank in the larger municipality of Bell Buckle, population four hundred. Here he met my mother, Mildred Freeman.

Mildred Freeman entered the world on February 4, 1909. She was the third in a family of five children born to John Knox Freeman, MD, and his wife, Ethel. Dr. Freeman was an old-fashioned country doctor in every sense of the term—the kind that no longer exists. He dealt with measles, gunshot wounds, births, deaths, and everything in between. As the only doctor in Bell Buckle and the surrounding communities, his door was always wide open. He treated everyone regardless of color, creed, or socioeconomic class.

In addition to owning the largest house in town, Dr. Freeman also owned six hundred acres of farmland. When patients were unable to pay their bills with money, he would accept sheep, cattle, or any suitable farm animal. On occasion, he was even paid with a bucket of molasses.

Bell Buckle was the home of Webb School, a highly regarded boarding school for boys, most of them from well-to-do families in Nashville. Dr. Freeman served as the school physician and, as such, was permitted to send two of his daughters, my mother, Mildred, and her older sister, Dorothy, to be educated alongside the young male students at Webb. The Freeman girls were not only the first females in the school, they would be the last ones for nearly fifty years; Webb did not become coeducational until 1973.

I wish I knew more about how my parents met, but it's always been something of a mystery to me. Somehow, Mildred and Claude came to be introduced in the early days of the Great Depression that followed the stock market crash in October 1929. They were married and moved from Bell Buckle to Nashville in 1932. My sister, Mildred, arrived in 1933. Eighteen months later, on September 27, 1934, I was born.

The Depression made life difficult for practically everyone in the country and in many other parts of the world. Without enough jobs or food to go around, most families barely scraped by—and some did not survive the crisis at all. Though I never realized it at the time, the Jarmans were quite poor. But we never went hungry. Fortunately, we lived only a train ride from my grandparents' large, comfortable house in Bell Buckle, where the pantry was always chock full of good things to eat. At least one weekend a month, we would visit my grandparents' home, and Mildred and I would spend summers there when school was out. It was a wonderful way to grow up.

With my grandfather, Dr. Freeman. 1946

I idolized my grandfather and would often accompany him on his numerous house calls. Sometimes I would sleep in his car overnight while he was waiting for a baby to be born. I also relished my visits to his farm, which was about ten miles away from his house. My mother's brother, James, and his wife, Alice, lived on my grandfather's farm and were in charge of managing it. It was there that I learned to ride horses, a skill that would not only come in handy later in Hollywood but would actually help shape my movie career.

I still remember the dusty tempered road that led to my grandfather's farm. There were few bridges in those days, and when it rained, the creeks would rise and we would have to wait until the water receded to continue our journey. On one of those occasions, a strange thing happened. My grandfather was whittling a piece of wood and dropping the shavings into the rushing water.

I asked him if I could borrow the knife so I could whittle a little too. He handed me the knife, and I cut a few twigs off a small piece of wood.

"Now, don't throw my knife into the water," he admonished. That thought had never entered my mind until he suggested it. Suddenly I found myself looking at him and, almost in slow motion, pitching the knife straight into the flooded creek. We were both astonished. He made me take off my shoes and wade into the knee-deep water to retrieve it. We never found it.

The fact that my grandfather was a doctor spared me many trips to the hospital. When I was six, I attempted to climb the mantelpiece over the fireplace in my parents' home, which consisted of a large slab of concrete. As I grasped it, the entire mantelpiece came crashing down on my left hand, severely damaging three of my fingers. A Nashville doctor wrapped gauze bandages around them and said they would be fine in a few weeks. That weekend we went to the country. When my grandfather saw my fingers, he immediately rushed me to the nearest hospital in Shelbyville (a town near Bell Buckle) and maneuvered me onto the operating table. He knew in a glance that two of the fingers were crushed and needed to be set. For the next six months, I did special exercises to regain strength and restore the full usage of my left hand, an early form of physical therapy. For each fifteen-minute exercise I performed, my grandfather would give me a nickel.

The lean years of the Depression eventually subsided, but life did not get much easier. No sooner had the country's financial crisis ended than we found ourselves facing more deprivation and hardship as the United States became involved in World War II. The Jarmans continued with our frequent visits to the country, but the mood had changed. Many troops were stationed in the Bell Buckle area, either in training or on maneuvers. The soldiers would stop to rest in my grandfather's yard. As they cooled themselves beneath the shade of an old tree, they would give me dimes to go and fill their canteens with water. Only twenty miles south of my grandfather's farm in Tullahoma was a prison camp for German POWs. Knowing it was there brought the war unsettlingly close to home.

My father was past the draft age, so he continued to work. In the early 1940s, he was employed as an accountant with the railroad. As the wartime demand for goods increased, he began working nights and weekends making tents for the military, in addition to his weekday job. For years, it seems I rarely saw my father. My main source of parental love and support was my mother.

I loved being read to by my mother. She not only told me stories at bedtime but would often read me a chapter from a novel in the morning before I headed off to school. She taught me to love reading, and she ignited my imagination through the power of words and illustrations. When I was little, *Bambi* was my favorite book, and I loved the Heidi series as well.

My fondness for books and stories soon evolved into a love for the movies. For those born in the second half of the twentieth century or later, it must be difficult to imagine what motion pictures meant to Americans in the 1930s and '40s. There were other forms of entertainment, of course. Most families had radios in their homes, and naturally, we had newspapers and magazines. Many people owned cars and lived within driving distance of some type of performance venue where they could see plays or music performed live. But there was nothing else like the movies.

For only twenty-five cents, you stepped into a dark palace and experienced a whole new world, projected right before your eyes, larger than life. You saw newsreels of the war in Europe and other news of the world, followed by cartoons, short musical films, Western or adventure serials, and the feature presentation. You could even stay and watch the whole show again without paying extra. It was a ticket to hours of excitement and a vital escape from the everyday. Our local theater in Nashville was the Belmont, only ten blocks away from our house.

During that time, most of the movies were war stories. My favorite movie actor was Dana Andrews. Perhaps I identified—or wished to identify—with his quiet strength. He always played a guy who could get tough if he needed to but was essentially honest and sincere. His screen persona was similar to the type Gregory Peck would later embody, the kind of man we'd all like to have for a father. Andrews's most memorable role to me was as Captain Harvey Ross in Lewis Milestone's *The Purple Heart,* released in 1944. That same year, he costarred with Gene Tierney in Otto Preminger's classic film noir *Laura.* I saw it first at the Belmont.

I also loved Roy Rogers movies. Being a boy, I was probably impacted the most by Westerns and war pictures, but I saw all kinds of films. The movies for me were a twice-weekly ritual, capped off by a double feature on Saturdays. Did this prepare me to be catapulted into the world of Hollywood? Of course not. Did it subconsciously plant the seed and guide me in that direction? I believe so. Clearly my interest in acting was the natural outgrowth of a lonely boy consumed by daydreams and cinema-inspired make-believe.

In those days, I never gave much thought to how the movies were made, never contemplated how difficult it must be to enact everything for the camera from every angle, over and over again, until it was just perfect. I knew nothing about the industry. The moguls who ran the studios, the screenwriters who created the material, the producers, the unions, the distributors, the gossip columnists, the critics . . . it may as well have existed on a different planet. I was just a kid enjoying a fantasy world.

Going to Hollywood and becoming a movie star never entered my mind; it seemed about as likely as building a rocket ship and traveling to the moon. The closest I had come was performing on the stage. At age eight, I was selected for my first acting part, the lead role in a play called *Walter, the Lazy Mouse* at Eakin School. In fifth grade, I played the title character in *Dr. Doolittle.* Performing came easily to me, and I soon joined the Nashville community theatre. It was an opportunity to learn acting and to escape into the same kind of alternate reality that the movies offered.

In February of 1945, we lived in a small rented house on 18th Avenue in Nashville. Our home had two bedrooms, one of which I shared with my sister. The family was still scrambling; by the time I was ten years old, we had moved seven times. The war had been raging full-force for about four years and was now consuming the Pacific as well as Europe. Life was hard for grown-ups, but I was a happy, carefree kid. I enjoyed my fifth-grade class at Eakin and was making good grades. I owned a bicycle, which I rode to school and to various friends' houses to play. It was a fairly typical childhood. Until Friday, February 14.

On that day, our class had a Valentine's Day celebration. At around two in the afternoon, I was helping take down the pink-and-red decorations when two strange men entered the classroom accompanied by Miss Maria Cage, the school principal. They seemed to notice me, and I noticed them, wondering to myself what they wanted. Shortly after they left the room, I was summoned to Miss Cage's office where both the men were waiting. I was introduced to a Mr. Brown and a Mr. Marchant. The men took turns asking me some general questions.

"What sports do you like?"

"Where in Tennessee do want to go to college?"

"Have you ever acted in any plays?"

Out of the blue, they asked if I had read a book called *The Yearling.*

"No, I haven't," I replied honestly. I had never even heard of it.

After talking with them for about fifteen minutes, the meeting ended with Mr. Marchant saying that he would call me later.

As I biked home in the frosty air, I pondered the strange encounter. What was it all about? I told my mother about it and mentioned that there might be a possibility of a visit from these mysterious men. At that point, Mildred arrived home and poured cold water on my intriguing news, as older sisters have a habit of doing.

"Those men are just building inspectors," she said. "They visited our classroom too." I decided to forget the whole thing and rode over to visit a friend who lived several blocks away.

While I was gone, Mr. Brown and Mr. Marchant knocked on our door. My mother told them I was gone, so they left. That could have been the end of it, but thirty minutes later, they called on the phone.

"Can Claude be brought back home, Mrs. Jarman?" they asked. "We have something very important to discuss with him." I was promptly tracked down and instructed to report home immediately. My two mystery visitors were waiting with my mother when I entered the house. Over the course of the next hour, I discovered that Mr. Brown was one of MGM's top directors, Clarence Brown, and Mr. Marchant was Jay Marchant, his production assistant. They were on a mission, they said, touring the South, searching for an unknown blonde boy to play the lead role in a movie version of *The Yearling*.

"Would you be interested in going to Hollywood for a screen test?" Mr. Brown asked.

"Sure" was my nonchalant reply. It all seemed so unreal and far-fetched to a cynical Depression kid. Daydreams and movies may have entranced me, but I knew the difference between fantasy and cold, hard reality. Things like overnight Hollywood fame just didn't happen to people like me.

Mr. Brown pulled out his camera and snapped a few still photos of me. With that, they departed but promised to be back in touch soon. I was convinced we would never hear from them again.

Photo that was sent to Sidney Franklin,
producer of *"The Yearling"*, February 19, 1945.

Saturday morning dawned grim and gray, and by afternoon, large, wet snowflakes had started to fall. Observing my usual Saturday ritual, I ensconced myself in the front row of the Belmont Theatre and settled in for a double feature. Around three o'clock, the manager (who knew his best customer by name) tapped me on the shoulder and whispered in my ear that I was wanted at home. My mother was waiting to tell me that Mr. Brown had requested my presence at the Hermitage Hotel in downtown Nashville.

Clarence Brown, I later found out, was piloting himself on this trip across the South. He had planned to search for other boys in Knoxville but was unable to fly there in the harsh weather conditions. So he decided to pursue our conversation further. My mother called my father, who was working downtown, and met me at the hotel. My father stayed in the adjoining room with Jay Marchant while I spent three hours with Brown that day. He told me the story of *The Yearling*, describing the setting and characters in the way only a seasoned film director can. "Jody is a lonely boy growing up in the Florida Everglades," I recall him telling me, "and the fawn he befriends becomes very important to him."

Brown watched and listened intently as I read several scenes from the script. He seemed to be interested in more than whether or not I was photogenic or if I could deliver a line believably—he wanted to know the kind of boy I was. Did I have patience and a lengthy attention span? Was I smart enough to comprehend the complexities of the character arc and the relationships? I nodded and understood the basics—especially the part about the fawn, since animals and the story of *Bambi* were close to my heart—but honestly, I grasped little of what Brown said that day. When we parted, there was the usual "We'll be back in touch." This time, I was starting to believe it.

Brown and Marchant departed for Knoxville the following morning. After about five days with no word, I gave up thinking about it and moved on with my life. My father and I laughed about the "Don't call us, we'll call you" expression the men had used, and we decided to let the whole thing go. My surprise was genuine when a call came from MGM the following week. In those days, movie studios didn't ask, they told. "Be ready to come to Hollywood next week for a screen test," they instructed.

A frenzy of questions and discussions arose at home. What about school? My father's job? Should my mother, who had never been more than fifty miles from Nashville in her life, drop everything to accompany me? Would Mildred come along? With less than a week to prepare and make the arrangements, it was finally decided that my father would take a two-week vacation from work, and we would both travel to California. We discussed it with my teacher, who prepared my lessons even though we had no idea where I would go to school.

In the days before the antitrust laws were enforced, studios owned their own theater chains. Our local MGM contact was Tom Detlich, the manager of the Loew's theatre in downtown Nashville, Loew's being the parent company of MGM. Obviously MGM did not have a Nashville office, so Mr. Detlich acted as my point person, in charge of making sure my travel was arranged and that I boarded the train safely.

On the appointed day, my father and I stepped aboard a night sleeper for Chicago, on the good old NC&StL. I loved trains and still do. Like movie theaters, trains added a dose of excitement to small-town life, especially in Tennessee, home to the world-famous "Chattanooga Choo-Choo." Though two of my uncles were railroad engineers and my father had also worked for the railroad, we could rarely afford to ride the trains. I used to sit and watch the locomotives chug through town, sounding their banshee whistles and trailing plumes of black smoke in their wakes. Sometimes I would place a penny on the tracks and watch in delight as the gigantic wheels of the engine pulverized it. Now I was riding the train across the country! I was too excited to sleep that night. Being on board a sleeper train thrilled me more than the idea of being in the movies.

The following morning, we arrived in Chicago. An MGM representative met us and took us on a brief tour of the city before we boarded the Santa Fe Chief, one of the premiere trains in the country back then, and powered along toward Los Angeles.

It took two nights and two days to reach LA. The stops en route were eye-opening for us: Kansas City, Albuquerque, Phoenix . . . the countryside was breathtaking. Stretches of sunbaked desert with craggy mountains in the distance gradually gave way to rows of palm trees and little Spanish-style houses with red clay roofs. We had reached our destination.

Another Metro ambassador greeted my father and me at the LA station and cheerfully drove us to the Washington Hotel in Culver City. MGM had been housing its out-of-town guests and new discoveries there since the studio's inception in 1924. A young Lucille LeSueur had stayed at the Washington Hotel in 1925 while Metro figured out what to do with her; they eventually renamed her Joan Crawford and the rest is history. But I didn't know any of that when my father and I checked in at the front desk. The hotel, with its slightly run-down grandeur, was just another escapade for a wide-eyed boy away from home for the first time.

Culver City has never been much to look at, the main attraction being the studios. There was Selznick International Pictures, with its white colonial facade (modeled on George Washington's home, Mount Vernon) seen at the beginning of Selznick classics like *Rebecca* and *Gone With the Wind*; the Hal E. Roach Studio, home of the Little Rascals, which no longer stands but at the time of my arrival was producing military training films; and finally, there was the daddy of them all, Metro-Goldwyn-Mayer. Dominating the landscape with the imposing insignia of Leo the Lion perched atop the sign, the massive, bustling offices and soundstages of MGM were a sight to behold.

We had no car, and MGM sent no car, so my father and I walked to the studio each day. From the hotel, it took about thirty minutes. Though they were always friendly and polite, the studio personnel treated me as just another kid taking a screen test. Probably dozens of young people shot tests for the studio each year, and in most cases nothing—no contracts or film roles—ever came of it. And this is precisely what I expected from my test: nothing. And that was fine with me. "Even if this movie doesn't pan out," I remember thinking, "at least I got a cross-country train trip out of it." When you're ten years old, it's all about the experience and the adventure.

My sense of adventure failed me after two weeks of waiting at the hotel with no word. No screen test. No Clarence Brown. MGM told us to be patient while Mr. Brown tested actresses for the role of

Mrs. Baxter. My dad's two-week vacation stretched into a thirty-day leave of absence.

Finally, after four weeks of hotel life and homesickness, I reported to MGM for my screen test. I'm not sure what I expected, but it wasn't quite what I had imagined. I was not even the focus of the long-awaited event—I was merely reading with various women to help decide which one would play my mother. First I enacted a scene with character actress Anne Revere and then with a younger blonde woman named Jacqueline White. The cavernous soundstage, the burning lights, and the glaring eye of the camera were imposing at first, but the set they had constructed (of the Baxter family kitchen) was homey, and I began to feel comfortable. For my first time before a camera on a film set, with script girls, assistants, hair and makeup artists, and various studio personnel hovering around, I felt surprisingly at ease—just a bit bewildered and unsure.

There was never a formal announcement of my fate, but after the screen test, Mr. Brown ("Clarence" to me by now) tipped off my father that I had the role. "If I were you, Mr. Jarman, I'd quit my job and devote my time to Claude's career." Looking back on it today, seventy years later, I still find it almost impossible to believe. I was going to be the star of a movie.

CHAPTER 2

Jody

By the early spring of 1945, Hollywood had weathered many storms. The industry had survived the transition from silents to talkies, the invention of Technicolor, the lean years of the Great Depression, and two world wars, and had cemented its reputation as the dream factory of the world. In 1941, techniques used in *Citizen Kane* and *The Maltese Falcon* ushered in a subversive new trend in filmmaking, the chiaroscuro-lit crime film, later to be known as film noir. The polished opulence of 1930s cinema had been replaced by a grittier realism born of World War II newsreels depicting atrocities on the battlefields and in the concentration camps.

Families were being broken and separated by the war, leading to a resurgence of family-friendly films. No studio cornered the market on family-friendly entertainment quite like Metro, home of the Andy Hardy and Lassie series. *Son of Lassie,* the sequel to *Lassie Come Home,* had recently been filmed in Canada using the new Technicolor Monopack system, allowing for a lighter camera that made location shooting easier. *National Velvet* had just been released to great acclaim, making a star of thirteen-year-old Elizabeth Taylor and resulting in a Best Director Academy Award nomination for Clarence Brown.

Brown, illustrious producer Sidney Franklin (the man behind *The Good Earth* and *Mrs. Miniver,* among other classics), and MGM were now striving to follow the success of *National Velvet* with *The Yearling,* another touching story about a young person's special bond with an animal. By 1945, *The Yearling* already had a star-crossed history. After purchasing rights to Marjorie Kinnan Rawlings's novel in 1938, MGM started preproduction on a film adaptation in 1941. Victor Fleming, fresh from his triumph *Gone with the Wind,* was directing. Spencer Tracy was signed to play the father, Anne Revere was the mother, and Gene Eckman, a young unknown boy from Atlanta, had been chosen for the lead role of Jody Baxter. The experience was a miserable failure. The Florida sun was relentlessly oppressive, and the humidity and mosquitoes made the locations unbearable. Tracy hated the role (and the heat), the boy grew too fast, the animals were uncooperative, and the world was engulfed in war. After three months, the production was shut down, and the cast and crew returned to Los Angeles in defeat.

Later, preeminent silent maestro King Vidor was assigned to the project, but nothing ever materialized from that effort. In late 1944, formidable studio head Louis B. Mayer decided to revive the project. Mayer was a man who loved a dollar and loathed waste; the money spent on the aborted *Yearling* attempts nagged at him. He was determined to get it back, plus a profit. Mayer knew he needed a top-notch director and one who could handle animals and children.

If Irving Thalberg was MGM's Boy Wonder, Clarence Brown was its Golden Child. Brown had earned his stripes directing Depression-era goddess Greta Garbo in some of her greatest films, both silent and talking. He had won Mayer's respect as a quiet, reliable worker with a gentle touch and a dedication to his craft. Brown spent the 1930s and early '40s directing Garbo and his favorite actress, Joan Crawford, in a string of profitable films. In 1943 and 1944, Brown made *The Human Comedy* and *National Velvet,* both artistic and financial successes for the studio and both featuring child actors. Mayer suspected that Brown was a natural for *The Yearling.*

Brown also considered himself a Southerner (having attended the University of Tennessee), and he knew exactly what to look for in Jody: a real Southern boy, one who embodied the character naturally and effortlessly. Brown also renovated the casting process by initiating a whole new method. Instead of the way MGM had gone about it the first time—running advertisements in local newspapers inviting fair-haired ten-year-old boys to audition *en masse* for talent scouts—he took charge of the hunt personally. An avid pilot, Brown flew himself and his assistant, Jay Marchant, to Memphis, Nashville, Knoxville, Atlanta, and Birmingham to find Jody.

In order to accomplish his mission without causing a stir, Brown employed a unique approach. Upon arriving in a city, his first stop was at the office of the school superintendent, where he would introduce himself and request an official letter that he could take to any local elementary school principal for permission to visit fifth- and sixth-grade classrooms. If he spotted a youngster he wished to interview, he would be able to do so. If he saw no boys who interested him, he would depart and no one would ever know he was there. This was the procedure that he followed when he arrived at Eakin School in Nashville at 2:45 on a Friday afternoon. He decided to take a quick look before flying off to his next destination in Knoxville. That last stop is the one that changed my life forever.

After my whirlwind discovery, screen test, and a few weeks of schooling at the MGM schoolhouse (more about that later), in mid-April I found myself boarding another train with my father—this one to Florida—where we would start filming. The train wound south through Atlanta and on to Jacksonville. I was unimpressed by the scenery on this trip. When you're a kid, a couple of months can feel like forever, and I had already gotten spoiled by living in Los Angeles. My enthusiasm was low as we traveled back through small Southern cities, all of which looked too similar to where I had come from. California was now in my veins.

From Jacksonville, we were transported by van to Ocala, a lazy little town in the Florida bush country, best known today for its horse-racing stud farms. Ten miles away is Silver Springs, with its world famous artesian springs and glass-bottom boats, now one of Florida's hottest vacation spots. In 1945, it was quiet and rustic.

The entire film company filled up the Silver Springs Motel, right across from the resort. My father and I were among the first to arrive. On the road outside the motel, an enterprising teenage boy had set up a fresh orange juice stand offering all you could drink for a quarter—a bargain I could not refuse but wish I had. I gulped cup after cup, oblivious to the acidity in fresh orange juice that my system was not used to. I ended up in the Ocala hospital for three days with severe stomach problems! Thankfully, I recovered in time to arrive on set the following Monday for my first day of filming.

The first scene we shot was in a buggy with my "Pa," Gregory Peck, whom I had never met until we arrived in Florida. His movie career had started with a bang, as he was nominated for a Best Actor Academy Award for his second film, *The Keys of the Kingdom*. Peck's star was on the rise. He had just wrapped production on the block-buster *Duel in the Sun* with Jennifer Jones when they hustled him down to Ocala to play Ezra "Penny" Baxter. Penny was an ideal pioneer father: loving, understanding, strong, and filled with folksy wisdom. The role suited Gregory Peck to a tee.

Greg was a joy to work with. "Hello, Jody" were his first words to me, and he called me Jody for the rest of the shoot. He wanted to establish a genuine rapport with me—a bond that would translate to a believable father–son dynamic on the screen—and he succeeded. He had recently become a father for the first time (his son Jonathan was born in 1944), and he was just as warm and kind as he appears in the film. Attentive to every detail, he was always on time and always prepared. And God, was he patient. Working with a raw young kid in his first picture (not to mention an untrainable young deer in its first picture) was no small challenge. Word has it that Spencer Tracy was unable to cope with such conditions in 1941, but I never once saw Greg angry or frustrated. Ever.

Loving times with my Pa (Gregory Peck)

We were in practically every scene together for ten months, experiencing every possible emotion, but he kept the mood cheerful. I remember a lot of laughing and joking. How lucky was I to play Gregory Peck's son in my first ever professional acting gig? After the film was released, we did two radio versions, not to mention attending premieres and events together. He was always the same genuinely kind man I met in Ocala.

Anne Revere, fresh from her role as Elizabeth Taylor's mother in *National Velvet* (and cast in the 1941 *Yearling* attempt), was initially considered to play "Ma" but was quite a bit older than Gregory Peck. For some reason, MGM settled on Jacqueline White, an unknown actress in her early twenties. Given the fact that Jody was eleven years old and Mrs. Baxter had already buried three children, a twenty-two-year-old woman was not exactly ideal for the part. But somehow she got it. Since most of her scenes took place indoors, Jacqueline had little to do in Florida. Somebody must have done the math, because when we returned to the studio in August, Miss White was replaced by Jane Wyman.

For me, making *The Yearling* was a trial by fire. From the front row of the Belmont Theater, movies had seemed like carefree make-believe worlds to me. What a rude awakening! Clarence Brown was a man who made films the painstaking, old-fashioned way—no shortcuts. From that very first day, he hovered like an overprotective mother lion, dictating my every move. He made sure I wore a straw hat whenever I was not on camera, as my sensitive skin burned easily and he was adamant that the actors wear no makeup. I also had strict orders to avoid Coca-Cola, my favorite drink, as Clarence was terrified I might break out in pimples. On a few occasions, I hid in the back of a property truck and enjoyed a forbidden Coke. Clarence and I took a walk most evenings to discuss the next day's shoot. He was anxious when we started because I was a bit stiff on camera, and I spoke all my lines in the same unnatural singsong voice. But I learned fast. Clarence gradually loosened up somewhat as he observed my progress.

Once May arrived, the Florida heat became unrelenting—the kind of steaming humidity that takes your breath away and saps the strength from your bones. In early July, the rains came and stayed. Buckets of rain would fall for days, drawing swarms of mosquitoes by the thousands. There were many days when not a scene or even a single frame of film was taken. We would sit in the trailer or under a tree, swat the bugs away, and watch the sky for a break in the clouds, then scramble to get a scene in. I soon became an expert at playing checkers.

When Clarence finally yelled "Action!" the process became even more frustrating. Brown was known to shoot a scene over and over again until he got exactly what he wanted. Add to that the tremendous pressure put on him to create something great (the *Los Angeles Times* had begun referring to *The Yearling* as "Metro's Folly") and turn a substantial profit, and you have a situation guaranteed to try any actor's patience. We would do the same scene ten, twenty, thirty times until it was perfect. And then Clarence would say, "Once more for Paris." There was one brief scene with the deer, myself, and Greg that took seventy-two takes to complete. I think the record-breaker was a scene where Jody opens the gate to a neighbor's yard and the fawn walks through. After around eighty takes, the deer finally nailed it. Greg later said that keeping our annoyance from showing was "probably the best acting we did in the picture."

The technology of the era slowed us down even further. Today's small, advanced equipment makes the job easier, but in the 1940s, acting in a film consisted mainly of endless waiting. The enormous Technicolor camera took forever to set up, and color film needed extra light. There were blazing arc lights and reflectors all over the place. Our cinematographer, Charles Rosher, had gotten his start shooting Mary Pickford films in the 1910s and won the first ever Academy Award for Best Cinematography for his work on F. W. Murnau's 1927 masterpiece *Sunrise*. Len Smith, his co-director of photography, was also a seasoned perfectionist. We were further blessed with art direction by the brilliant Cedric Gibbons. Rosher and Gibbons would both receive Oscars for their work on *The Yearling*.

The sound problem proved to be the most exasperating, at least for Clarence Brown. In the wilds of the Ocala National Forest, the crackle of every branch or leaf was picked up, often ruining an otherwise perfect take. After completing filming, the following January we spent six weeks looping most of the dialogue for the exterior scenes shot in Florida. This so enraged Clarence that when we made *Intruder in the Dust* a few years later in Oxford, Mississippi, he shot every scene with open mike solely to get a sound track. He then returned to Culver City and looped the entire film.

We also strained to work within school laws and regulations, which caused more delays. Minors have to be schooled for a certain number of hours every day, either in a schoolroom or on set with a tutor. This was fairly strictly enforced, though sometimes my tutor would look the other way for an additional fifteen minutes of shooting time. Most days I received my education in ten and fifteen-minute segments. When there was a pause between camera setups, all the other actors would get to relax and take a break. Not me. I would hear my director order, "Jody, go to school." Some days, the entire production had to shut down from two to four so I could get my remaining two hours of school in before the end of day. My schedule was brutal.

Compounding an already difficult shoot was yet another challenge: what King Vidor had called "that damn fawn problem." Finding a deer the size of a true yearling was easy. But young fawns grow rapidly and lose their white spots practically overnight. This meant early scenes involving the fawn had to be shot quickly, and a reserve of baby deer was needed on standby. MGM sent word around the Florida bush country, offering money to any of the natives who brought in a fawn. The cutest and most photogenic was three days old and had been found near a forest fire missing his mother. We named him Bambi, and he grew to be a yearling. Fortunately for us all, I had a natural rapport with animals, just like my character. Bambi would actually sit for hours in my lap with his legs folded beneath him. Incredible.

There were about five main deer used in the film, but Bambi was the star. When MGM sent me to New York and Chicago for three weeks promoting *The Yearling*'s release, Bambi came along. There I was, onstage every day for a week at Radio City Music Hall, towing a full-grown deer on a leash.

The company spent about four months in Silver Springs. We worked long days and returned to the un-air-conditioned motel at night to swelter. We spent our leisure time exploring the Silver River in the famous glass-bottom boats. I vividly recall seeing countless varieties of tropical fish, turtles, snake, and water moccasins beneath the water. The five-foot-long rattlesnakes and deadly coral snakes on the shore also fascinated me.

With Bambi, my favorite fawn.

I befriended an interesting man named Ross Allen, who ran a reptile exhibit at Silver Springs. Each morning, he would enter a pen filled with a hundred snakes. Of the slithering reptiles, he selected about ten rattlers, grabbing them one at a time. He pried open their mouths, positioned their inch-long fangs over a glass, and collected the deadly venom that oozed forth. (The venom is used as an antidote for snake bites.) Unsurprisingly, Ross had been bitten at least once and was missing half of a thumb. Ross also hunted alligators, and my dad and I often accompanied him. Out on his boat in the dark of night, Ross would shine the light on his helmet, and when he saw two eyes staring at him, he would slink into the depths of the river and swim toward the eyes. Transfixed by the light, the alligators remained motionless as Ross silently approached. Ross's life depended upon his ability to clamp the gator's jaws shut before the animal attacked. Exciting times in the brush.

In mid-August, after four months of grueling, blistering sun and heat, armies of mosquitoes, and enough rain to drown us all, we left Florida for California. The company plan was to reconvene at the studio in two weeks to begin filming mostly interior scenes.

Just before we broke camp, I had jumped a major hurdle: my first real crying scene. Jody has to shoot his beloved "Flag" the fawn, to put the deer out of his misery after it had been shot by his mother. Though no animals were hurt during the making of the film, they tied down the deer in its final scene, so it would writhe and struggle and appear to be in pain. My ability to cry—not just cry, but sob—was crucial to the entire film. Without believable tears from Jody, there would be no dramatic impact and the whole story would fall flat.

Clarence talked to me for an hour the night before, using my love of animals to tug at my heartstrings. "Think of this poor deer," he told me. "This is your best friend, the pet you have raised from a baby." I don't know if the sadness of the scene or the pressure of everyone watching me did the trick, but the tears came rolling down my cheeks in rivulets. I was absolutely petrified, and I found myself bawling. "When Clarence got that kid to cry," Gregory Peck later recalled, "it changed the whole nature of the picture." Not only that, it generated a collective sigh of relief from the entire production company.

From Jacksonville, my father and I took a train to Nashville to pick up my mother and sister; the family was relocating to Hollywood—an amazing turn of events when you consider that my father's visit to the 1933 Chicago World's Fair was the only time any of us had been out of Tennessee. I stepped off that train looking like a hippie before there was such a term. My hair had grown to my shoulders, and I was barefoot. The soles of my feet were two giant calluses—squeezing them into shoes was an impossibility. After four months of running shoeless through the Everglades, I could step on thorns and not feel a thing.

We retraced the route we had taken in February—sleeper to Chicago, then the Santa Fe Chief to Los Angeles—but this time around, I was a valuable contract player. An MGM sales rep picked us up at the Chicago station in a limousine and took us on a brief tour of the city. Instead of the Los Angeles station, this time we disembarked at Pasadena. I was later told that this was the preferred stop for "movie people" since they could avoid fans and photographers. Needless to say, that was not a problem for the Jarman family.

It certainly felt like we had shot an entire film in Florida. But, incredibly, *The Yearling* was only halfway finished. All of the interior scenes and some of the exterior scenes were still to be shot. And all of the sequences with Ma Baxter had to be reshot with a new actress. Jane Wyman stepped into Jaqueline White's place when we regrouped in early September, and right away it seemed as if she had always been there.

Jane had been at Warner Bros. for most of her career. For over ten years, the studio squandered her dramatic talents on chorus-girl parts or lightweight comedies like *Brother Rat,* where she met her future husband Ronald Reagan in 1938. She had finally been given a meaty breakthrough role in *The Lost Weekend* with Ray Milland in 1945, and though the film had not yet been released, the industry was starting to realize that Jane was more than just a pretty face.

with Jane Wyman and Gregory Peck.

When she started working on *The Yearling*, Jane was still married to Reagan and was working and taking care of their two children, Maureen and Michael, while her husband was stationed overseas. A few years later, she divorced the future president. So much for being First Lady. The future First Lady was right under our nose at that time—the young Nancy Davis was a contract player at MGM.

Jane was a breath of fresh air on the set, always laughing and full of life. She was an upbeat lady, and we became friends easily, though not in the same way I had bonded with Gregory Peck. In the film, Ory Baxter is a woman who suppresses her emotions and shows her affection toward her husband and son by being the strict disciplinarian of the family. Because there were virtually no warm scenes between us, Jane and I never grew very close. Still, we remained in contact for years. In the 1980s, after I had relocated to the San Francisco area, I used to drive out and visit Jane at Inglenook Vineyards, where they filmed her TV series *Falcon Crest*.

On the set with Jane Wyman and Gregory Peck.

Before shooting interiors in Culver City, we took a much-needed break and moved production to Lake Arrowhead, about ninety miles northeast of Los Angeles. A whole town had been constructed just for the film (something that would never happen today). The cast stayed in a hotel on the other side of the lake and took a boat across to the set each day. On most mornings, Clarence, who had commandeered a rowboat, insisted I accompany him as he rowed across the lake. My mother and sister came up, and it was like a family vacation. Well, a star-studded family vacation. Greg Peck brought his wife Greta, and Ronald Reagan even came up to visit. When I met Mr. Reagan, he looked quite handsome in his Army uniform and seemed very happy. We were all in a good mood—World War II had just ended.

After our lakeside holiday, some of the most challenging work lay ahead: the sequences that formed the emotional core of the film. In other words, more tears for Jody. October and November were spent on the MGM soundstage, shooting scenes that built to the climactic moment when Jody shoots Flag.

The first scene was after my Pa had been "snake-bit" and I turned to our neighbors, the Forresters, for help. When the five Forrester boys appeared on their front porch, I ran up to them in tears, shouting, "Pa—he's snake-bit!" Forrest Tucker, who played Lem Forrester, was so shocked to see me crying that he was unable to say his lines. This did not please Clarence, who assailed poor Forrest with a torrent of harsh language. But we did eventually get that scene in the can.

Several days later, we shot the emotional sequence where Jody says a final good-bye to his crippled young friend Fodderwing. Chill Wills, who played Fodderwing's older brother Buck, stands beside me at the foot of the boy's deathbed. "He'll not hear, but speak to him," says Buck. I break into tears as Buck softly explains how Fodderwing had named Jody's deer "Flag." Chill and I were both crying and had been for several takes. It was six o'clock on a Saturday, and we had to complete the scene that evening. The whole crew was scheduled to leave the next morning to a new location at Lake Arrowhead. It was quitting time for everyone, especially me. As a minor, I was not allowed to work overtime. But everyone kept going—we had to. After an additional thirty minutes, we finally completed the emotional scene. As I was headed to my dressing room, the producer, Sidney Franklin, who had made one of his rare visits to the set, stopped me and handed me a $5 bill. Finishing that scene had saved the company a small fortune.

My most emotional scenes were when Jody leads Flag out to the woods and tells him to "never come back," and later, when he lashes out at his parents after Ma shoots the deer. Pa tells Jody, "You've got to finish him." I still remember my lines. My first response is to my mother: "You done it on purpose. You always hated him!" Then to my father: "You went back on me, you told her to do it. I hate you! I hope you die! I hope I never see you again!" With dialogue like that, it was easy to get emotional. Once more, the tears flowed.

my 11th birthday on the set at the studio with Clarence Brown, Gregory Peck and Sidney Franklin.

Every sequence Clarence shot followed essentially the same pattern: first the overall long shot, then the medium shot, followed by over-the-shoulder shot, and finally the close-up. Any sensible, sea-soned actor would know better than to give his best performance in a scene with his back to the camera. Later on I learned this lesson, but not on this day. By the end of the shoot, I was drained and exhausted, with barely enough tears left for the final close-up.

When I got home that night, I fell into bed. That was just about the time that my sister, Mildred, came down with whooping cough. The studio doctor was alarmed and suggested moving me and my father to a bungalow at the Beverly Hills Hotel. After about a week, it became apparent that we had moved too late; I had also contracted whooping cough. These days, babies are vaccinated for it, but back then, it was a serious and highly contagious threat to children. I went back home, and for six weeks, I suffered in bed, losing ten pounds as a result. Somehow, every morning I found the strength to get up and go to the studio. The production could not wait for me to recover, and we had to keep shooting. Many times we had to reshoot a scene because of my persistent coughing. It was hard work for only $150 a week!

I eventually recuperated and shot my fifth and final scene that required tears: when Jody runs away and nearly starves to death. After everything I had been through, that may have been the easiest scenario to bring to life.

With Christmas on the horizon, life improved considerably. We could see the light at the end of the tunnel. In early January 1946, main production on *The Yearling* was wrapped. We still had to return to Florida for a month (mostly for long shots of the surroundings), but Clarence Brown did not go. Chester Franklin, Sidney's brother, directed the various shots. When we returned to California, the cast spent several more weeks looping dialogue. The post-production and editing took so long that the film was not ready for release until December 1946. The entire production had taken one solid year.

When I look back on it, I realize that nothing else in my life after *The Yearling* experience ever came close to being that difficult. When we started shooting, I was ten. When the picture was released, I was twelve. I had grown three inches taller but still weighed less than one hundred pounds. I had gone from a movie-watching kid in Tennessee to a movie star in Hollywood. How did it happen? I basically *was* Jody. I was placed in the proper setting, guided by a master director, and assisted by accomplished talent, and fortunately for everyone, I responded accordingly. I lived the part.

After being called Jody for so long on the set, I got used to answering to that name. Before *The Yearling* was released in 1947, there was practically no one in the United States named Jody, which is a diminutive of the Hebrew name Judea. Because of *The Yearling*, the popularity of Jody skyrocketed for both boys and girls. There was a young male character named Jody on the 1960s TV series *Family Affair*, a doll named Jody in the early 1970s, and around the same time, a young actress named Alicia Christian Foster was given the stage name of Jodie Foster. But my Jody was the first one in popular culture.

CHAPTER 3

A Deer in the Headlights

B ack in Hollywood, I was the new kid on the MGM lot. I was now a contract player, paid the standard salary of $150 per week. At twelve, I was earning more than my father; the studio paid him $100 per week to be my guardian. That was considered a fairly decent income in 1945 but not enough for a mansion in Beverly Hills. Let's just say our leap to California was a lateral move from our modest home in Nashville—a one-bedroom house in Culver City with a rollaway in the living room.

Every morning, my father and I would take the twenty-minute walk to the studio, past the home of Robert "Little Beaver" Blake, star of the *Red Ryder* Western movies. As I approached the side-street that dead-ended at the East Gate, on the left stood the Irving Thalberg Building, named after the talented and beloved Hollywood executive who died a very early death of heart failure at the age of thirty-seven. All the top studio executives had their offices there: L. B. Mayer, casting guru Benny Thau, studio "fixer" Eddie Mannix, and cream-of-the-crop producers like Joe Pasternak, Arthur Freed, and Jack Cummings.

Across the street on the right was the parking lot reserved for the high-level executives, protected at all times by the MGM police force. Park there at your own risk. Even more exclusive was the right to enter the East Gate, past Officer Keating (the gatekeeper for decades), and park on the studio lot itself. Cars allowed to pass usually contained the likes of Clark Gable, Robert Taylor, or Van Johnson. A waving hand and, if you were lucky, a smiling face would emerge from the Cadillacs and Lincoln Continentals, and the bevy of autograph seekers who stood waiting on the corner would squeal in ecstasy.

Like my father, I tended to befriend the film-industry workers with the menial, behind-the-scenes jobs. These folks were the salt of the earth—no egos, no attitudes. My favorite guy on the MGM lot was a man named Bob who ran the shoeshine stand and newsstand next to the studio barber shop, just outside the commissary. Bob loved me. He always piled free magazines into my arms, never letting me pay him a cent. The friendly faces on the studio lot gave MGM a small-town feel. Everything you needed was right there. Stars like Robert Taylor could be spotted in the barber-shop chairs first thing in the morning. Instead of shaving at home, they came to work and let professional barbers give them a shave before they visited the makeup department.

They'd get a shoeshine, grab a copy of the *Hollywood Reporter,* and head to the set. It was like a glamorous version of Mayberry, USA.

By the time all production work on *The Yearling* was complete, I was in the sixth grade. M-G-M had a little two-room schoolhouse right on the lot. About twelve to sixteen students attended at that time; when I came back to the studio in 1950, there were none. Such was life in the final heyday of the studio system. A rotating crop of kids would come and go, depending on what films were being shot and screen tests made. My regular classmates included superstar-to-be Elizabeth Taylor, singing and dancing sensation Jane Powell, and resident "cute kid" Dean Stockwell.

Dean was always a bit distant and withdrawn from the rest of us. I didn't know him well enough to discover if he was troubled or simply introverted, but he never seemed as carefree or sociable as the others. Liz Taylor was the unofficial queen of the class. She was a mature fifteen, and she seemed light years ahead of the rest of us. Beautiful, popular, and kind, she was a charming young lady when I knew her, which was just before her fame skyrocketed. She was nurturing an obsession with Katharine Hepburn and used to flutter around the lot doing impressions of Kate in *Stage Door.* "The calla lilies are in bloom again!"

With Roddy McDowell and Elizabeth Taylor.

With Roddy McDowell and Jane Powell.

Jane was just as she appeared in her films: cute, bubbly, and down-to-earth. She was more of a regular kid than Elizabeth Taylor. Jane was just starting out in the movies after a successful career singing on the radio, and she seemed totally unaffected by Hollywood.

Elizabeth Taylor's 18th Birthday surrounded by classmates in 1950.

Margaret O'Brien was MGM's biggest child star at that time, and she had her own private tutor—though she did show up at the schoolhouse for recess every day. Later, in its July 1948 issue, *Modern Screen* printed a story about Margaret's crush on me: "Your baby's gone and done it! She's cut off her pigtails and fallen for Claude Jarman Jr." If it was true, she never made me aware of it. Margaret was a very quiet girl. In later years, we reunited and became good friends. As I got to know her better, I came to see that, like most soft-spoken and reserved people, she never seemed entirely comfortable in the spotlight. I suspect her mother and her aunt played a big role in her pursuit of stardom.

Margaret O'Brien presenting me with the
Parents Magazine Award in 1947.

With my wife Katie and Margaret O'Brien
at the Academy Awards in 1998.

At the premiere of *"The Yearling"* with my sister
Mildred and my parents in December 1946.

I, on the other hand, was a rarity in Hollywood: a kid actor whose parents had not pushed him into it. This is probably why I went as far as I did, because I was a natural, like Clarence Brown wanted. It's also probably why I could take Hollywood or leave it—I had no desperate need for stardom to prove my worth to a demanding parent who conditioned their child to equate fame with love. But at that time, I was still trying out the Hollywood life and enjoying it.

Getting an education at the world's top movie studio was far superior to regular school. Every student was required to be in the schoolhouse from 9:00 a.m. to 12:00 p.m., Monday through Friday. We had a fifteen-minute recess at 10:30—during which ping-pong was the game of choice—and at noon, class was dismissed, all the kids taking off in different directions. Every week, we all had to participate in a challenging exercise: each of us was required to speak before the class for five minutes about one subject. It could be any subject we desired—an item we had read in the newspaper, a movie we had seen, a trip we had taken. Five minutes is a long time to keep an audience interested. We all struggled with it, but Liz was probably the most successful. When it came to holding an audience in the palm of her hand, nobody took a backseat to Elizabeth Taylor.

We had more fun and shorter hours than most schoolchildren, but we also had a small student body and more personal attention from the teacher. All in all, it was not a bad way to learn. I find it disappointing that all the kids were bright, but most of them never attended college. Why go away to school when highly-paid career opportunities are yours for the taking right there on the studio lot?

My fondest memory of the MGM school days was the afternoon we took a very Hollywood field trip: a personal appearance at a war bond drive. A big Greyhound bus collected Jane Powell, Elizabeth Taylor, Elizabeth's older brother Howard, me, and my sister, Mildred, and drove us to Twentieth Century Fox, where we picked up Roddy McDowall, and headed to Bakersfield for the bond rally.

At the time, Roddy was working with Liz and Jane on the MGM musical *Holiday in Mexico,* but he was under contract at Fox. Roddy had actually briefly been considered for my role in *The Yearling,* before Clarence took over and insisted on an unknown. He was a bit older than the rest of us and made us laugh with his more sophisticated, polished British wit. Elizabeth Taylor, in particular, was very fond of him, and they remained close friends for the rest of their lives.

We all worked hard during the week, but on Sundays, we would play. Future *Forbidden Planet* star Anne Francis was another young MGM contract player at the time, and she sometimes joined in our social events, as did Amparin Iturbi, niece of musical sensation Jose Iturbi. Jose was a Spanish musical conductor who MGM turned into a movie star. He played what they used to refer to as the "Latin lover" type in films with Jeanette MacDonald and Jane Powell.

Back then, Jane's father ran a little soda fountain. We would meet there and gorge on banana splits, or get together on a vacant lot and have a big football game with Dean Stockwell and his brother Guy, or head up to Pacific Palisades for a party—the spontaneous, innocent kind of fun preteens and young teenagers used to have before the technology revolution.

Looking back, it almost feels like a dream. Like most dreams, it was too good to last. Within two or three years, we would each go our separate ways. Some would ascend the ranks of stardom, while others would struggle with that difficult transition from child to adult on-screen.

But in the late 1940s, we were just a handful of very fortunate kids. I may have been the luckiest of all, plucked from obscurity in Tennessee and dropped into the glamour factory of Metro-Goldwyn-Mayer at that magical moment in time. I got to enjoy the company of some of the world's most celebrated performers before Oscars, maturity, sophistication, and adult responsibilities weighed them down. It was as glorious as it was fleeting.

When I first signed my Metro contract just before making *The Yearling*, producer Sidney Franklin did what all studios did with fresh new talent. He signed me up for dramatic training. Located just inside the East Gate was the studio of Lillian Burns, drama coach to the stars (and wife of director George Sidney at the time). A tiny woman with an exuberant demeanor, Lillian was a talented and fascinating presence. "A painter can go into a room alone and paint a picture," she used to say. "But an actor needs an audience, and he needs his talent developed and directed."

I loved her and admired her dedication to the craft. She helped me prepare for the most terrifying performance of my life: the year I recited the Lord's Prayer to 15,000 onlookers—and to the entire world via live radio broadcast—at the Hollywood Bowl Easter Sunrise service (a Hollywood tradition since 1921). She never heckled or criticized; she instilled me with confidence by encouraging and supporting. She was an outspoken advocate for actor training and had a devoted following. Over the years, I would see Debbie Reynolds, Lucille Ball, and Nancy Davis, among others, in her packed waiting room.

All minors were required to spend every free minute in school when not rehearsing or filming. Due to my strict 9-to-6 schedule, working on my training with Lillian was a challenge. I ended up slipping into the lot at 8:00 a.m. and working with Lillian until nine. Then begin the official day. Lillian was a wonderful coach, but her penchant for the theatrical was antithetical to Clarence Brown's demand for natural realism. Some cynics on the *Yearling* set commented that Lillian injected all the high drama into my soul, only to have Clarence wring out every drop.

Somewhere between the influences of Clarence and Lillian, I managed to develop an acting style that seemed to work. After *The Yearling,* I was rushed right into *High Barbaree,* a sentimental drama starring the screen's hottest new duo, Van Johnson and June Allyson. Though it was edited and ready before *The Yearling,* Clarence insisted it be released later, so that his masterpiece would be my debut film.

In *High Barbaree,* I played Van Johnson's character as a kid in several lengthy flashback sequences. Makeup artist Jack Dawn and his crew had a field day in their attempt to make me resemble the freckled and wavy-haired star. When Van Johnson caught his first glimpse of my comically curled hair and painted-on Howdy-Doody freckles, he declared "I never looked like *that!*"

Van Johnson was a character. I used to observe him in the commissary. He always piled food on his tray and had his assistant pay for it, as Van never carried any pocket money. Decades later, he was revealed to be gay, but none of us had any inkling at that time.

People tend to forget how popular he was; he was a massive star and a national sensation. Young women went so wild for his all-American looks, they got a little hysterical. Watching the bobby-soxers swooning for his autograph outside the MGM gates was like witnessing a precursor to Beatlemania.

In her autobiography, June Allyson (who used to accompany Van on studio-arranged "dates") remembered, "Some nights were so bad we didn't dare leave the studio. When they started getting really rough—trying to tear clothes and yank hair—Van simply went into hiding." All this admiration did not make Van egotistical, but it did give him tremendous self-confidence. He always treated me with a great deal of professional respect, although, because I played him as a child, we had no scenes together. All my scenes were with Joan Wells, Thomas Mitchell, and the special bicycle that I had spent four weeks practicing on, as I did some fancy trick riding in the film. Joan Wells had played Eulalie, the little girl Jody threw a potato at in *The Yearling*, so we had already established a rapport.

Familiar character actor Thomas Mitchell is probably best known as Uncle Billy in the holiday classic *It's a Wonderful Life*, which he had just wrapped before starting *High Barbaree*. In our film, he played my Uncle Thad. Thomas holds a special distinction: he was the first fellow actor I encountered who attempted to deliberately upstage me. During a scene where his character hugged mine, I could not help but notice that—every single time we shot it—Thomas hugged me in a way so that my face was hidden from the camera, so I didn't steal a second of his camera time! As a kid, I found it hard to believe that a grown-up man would do that. It was my first lesson in Hollywood egos.

But *High Barbaree* was a fun experience. Of course, after *The Yearling*, anything seemed fun and easy. All the hard work was finally ready to pay off, though. Clarence Brown's precious project about a boy and his deer was just about to be released to the public.

"You should retire," Hedda Hopper told me when *The Yearling* was screened. "Quit show business now, because you'll never top this film's success or find a greater role." In a way, she was right. Hopper was one of the most powerful columnists in the industry. Like her archrival, Louella Parsons, Hopper's Hollywood column was syndicated in newspapers across the nation, and her words could make or break the stars. She had seen countless young actors come and go.

On December 18, the world premiere of *The Yearling* was held at the iconic Carthay Circle Theatre on San Vicente Boulevard in Los Angeles. Though it was razed in 1969, the Spanish cathedral–style landmark so dominated its surroundings that today the area is still referred to as Carthay Circle—the name of the theater that stood there decades ago.

The red carpet was rolled out like it hadn't been for years. This was the first major movie premiere after the end of World War II, and people finally felt like they could pull out all the stops and celebrate, without wartime rationing and restrictions. As Metro held most of its premieres on the east coast, *The Yearling* was the first MGM film to premiere outside of New York since *Gone With the Wind* held its gala Atlanta debut in 1939.

It was a big night for me. Searchlights, limousines, formal gowns and tuxedos, rows of bleachers packed with cheering fans, the press, and celebrities galore greeted me as I arrived with my family. Of course, L. B. Mayer, Clarence Brown, Greg Peck, and Jane Wyman were there in high spirits, but a Hollywood who's-who turned up too: Lana Turner, Ava Gardner, Red Skelton, Judy Garland, Vincente Minnelli, Elizabeth Taylor, Margaret O'Brien . . . as the *Los Angeles Times* printed the next day, "It was quite a turnout for a little boy and a fawn." Even the Navy was there, as a portion of proceeds from the event went to a naval charity for children in Guam. But on this night, I was the big star, and all eyes were on me.

At the premiere of *"The Yearling"* with Margaret O'Brien and L.B. Mayer

On a personal appearance tour at The Radio City Music Hall with Bambi in 1947.

I had seen the film once at a private screening but never publicly. The lights dimmed, and there I was on an enormous screen, in virtually every frame of film. And, to my surprise, the audience reacted with effusive enthusiasm. I could see and hear those around me laughing, weeping, and applauding like a thunderstorm when it was over. The moment the theater lights came up, I was the man of the moment. Suddenly, all of Hollywood knew me and wanted to hug me! We had done it, Clarence and all of us. *The Yearling* was received as an instant classic.

Bosley Crowther, the notoriously difficult-to-please *New York Times* critic, pronounced *The Yearling* a success, claiming it provided "such a wealth of satisfaction as few pictures ever attain." *Life* magazine ran a four-page spread on *The Yearling,* naming it "the picture of the week," and *Los Angeles Times* critic Edwin Schallert selected it as the best picture of the year.

All of our performances were praised, and most reviewers considered the film to be the greatest acting work both Peck and Wyman had ever done. And that was just the United States.

The popularity of the simple story of a boy and his fawn soon spread across the Atlantic and was embraced by the UK. The premiere in Leicester Square received a standing ovation. The *Sunday Express* called *The Yearling* "clearly one of Hollywood's best efforts," and *Kine Weekly* described it as *"The Good Earth, Huckleberry Finn,* and *Bambi* rolled into one."

I knew we had made something special, but at the time, I was unaware of the reviews. Early on in the process, Clarence Brown had advised me, "Never read your own publicity," and I took this advice very seriously (and literally). If I saw my name in print, I averted my eyes, refusing to glance at a single word. I may have gone overboard, but it probably served me well. Looking back now, I see that Hedda Hopper told her readers that I gave Gregory Peck a run for his money, and other powerful columnists predicted great fame for me, declared me "an actor to be reckoned with," and on and on. But I never believed the hype because I never read it.

After the premiere, the studio marketing team shipped me off to New York (two weeks) and Chicago (one week) to promote the film. During its run at Radio City Music Hall—known for the daily appearance of the famed Rockettes—I appeared twice a day on stage with Flag the fawn (a.k.a. Bambi), now a fully grown animal, antlers and all. Can you imagine sending a kid to Radio City Music Hall trailing a live deer on a leash? I felt a little like Kong, the eighth wonder of the world. While in town, I also gave numerous interviews at radio stations and various movie magazine offices, most of which were headquartered in Manhattan.

My father accompanied me, along with my tutor, Vic Griffith, Frank Liggett, who was in charge of Bambi, and someone from the studio publicity department. We all stayed at the Astor Hotel near Times Square. Though I was thrilled to be in New York City for the first time, it was all very overwhelming. I found it hard to enjoy myself because everything was moving much too fast for me. A year and a half earlier, I had been a normal kid living a quiet life in Nashville.

Now my world had turned upside down, and I was clinging on for dear life. As challenging as making *The Yearling* was, it had been a fulfilling experience, a private group effort. Filming scenes for Clarence's camera was intimate and comfortable. The post-movie hype was the part that tripped me up.

Stepping up on that stage at Radio City was truly terrifying. All eyes were on me, and I was beginning to feel like a traveling freak show. The rising doubts and dissatisfactions all came to a head one day when I found myself walking down Fifth Avenue with a deer on a leash at five o'clock in the afternoon. The noise, the traffic, the gawking pedestrians, the frightened animal—I knew how poor Bambi felt. I too was a deer in the headlights.

On that day, I knew that being a Hollywood movie star was not for me. You either learn to love it or hate it. At that moment, I hated it. I realized that I had boarded a train I couldn't stop. It was not within my power to change the course of my life at that time, but I knew I would someday. I would step out of the limelight and forge my own path.

CHAPTER 4

Oscars, Horses, and Women

The Oscars. Ever since the first Academy Awards ceremony in 1929, that gold statuette has been surrounded by hype and hope. Like the black bird in *The Maltese Falcon,* Oscar is "the stuff that dreams are made of." The 1947 awards—honoring films released in 1946—were special for several reasons. It was the first time the event was held at the cavernous 6,700-seat Shrine Auditorium in downtown Los Angeles. It was hosted (for the second and last time) by legendary comedian Jack Benny, broadcast nationwide via ABC radio, and open to the ticket-buying public for the first time. It also happened to be an exceptional year for movies. Films nominated include *The Best Year of Our Lives* with Fredric March and Myrna Loy, *The Razor's Edge* with Tyrone Power and Gene Tierney, Jimmy Stewart's favorite of his films, *It's a Wonderful Life,* and *Henry V,* featuring Laurence Olivier in the title role.

For me, this was a very special Oscars—my film debut was being honored by the most prestigious award in the industry. Competition was stiff, but *The Yearling* received six nominations including Best Picture, Clarence Brown for Best Director, Gregory Peck for Best Actor, and Jane Wyman for Best Actress. My father was tipped off that I should be ready to respond on stage; I might be given a special award. I had no idea what would happen.

The overwhelming favorite to win that year was *The Best Year of Our Lives,* a poignant, sentimental drama detailing the lives of three soldiers returning from World War II and their difficult adjustments to civilian life. As predicted, the film did sweep the major awards: Best Picture, Fredric March for Best Actor, and Harold Russell, an actual veteran who had lost both hands while making an army training film, won Best Supporting Actor as well as an honorary Oscar. But *The Yearling* was not overlooked by the Academy. Charles Rosher's remarkably natural Technicolor photography was rewarded with an Oscar for Best Cinematography, and Cedric Gibbons—who had not only won the Oscar five times (on his way to a career total of eleven Oscars), but had designed the gold statue himself—took home his sixth for *The Yearling*'s art direction.

I, of course, had no experience with the Oscars. I had never even listened to the ceremony on the radio. Thank God for my sessions with Lillian Burns. When my name was announced as the recipient of the award for Most Outstanding Child Actor of 1946, I was able to deliver a brief thank-you speech without screwing it up. In fact, I thanked Lillian in my acceptance speech, right along with Sidney Franklin and Clarence. The young lady who presented me with my Oscar was the first recipient of the special Academy Juvenile Award, and the biggest child star of all time—Shirley Temple. It was a thrilling moment. A panel of the greatest artists and technicians in the film industry had decided that my performance as Jody was worthy of the highest accolade. At twelve, I could barely process or believe such praise. Up on the stage, I said, "This is about the most exciting thing that can happen to anybody," but the full significance of the award escaped me.

At the Academy Awards with Shirley Temple in 1947.

The Oscar itself was a little less than half the size of a regular statuette. After Shirley won the award in 1935, the Academy honored eleven other child actors with this special prize over the next twenty-six years. I was in good company. Judy Garland, Mickey Rooney, Deanna Durbin, and Margaret O'Brien had also received mini-Oscars, and in 1961, Hayley Mills was the final recipient. When young Patty Duke won Best Supporting Actress for her work in *The Miracle Worker* in 1963, the juvenile award was discontinued. Patty's performance had convinced the Academy—and the world—that youths could compete right alongside adults and win. In the ensuing years, ten-year-old Tatum O'Neal and eleven-year-old Anna Paquin would receive full-size Oscars.

As proud as I was to own the juvenile Oscar, I must admit: compared to a regular Academy Award, it looked rather puny. Shirley Temple and I both ended up living in the Bay Area and would run into each other occasionally. About thirty years ago, she remarked that she felt embarrassed displaying such a tiny statuette. "I think we deserve a regular one like every other recipient," she told me. Several months later, I saw Shirley's picture in the newspaper receiving a full-size Oscar from the Academy president, so I wrote to the Academy asking for one too. Their initial reaction was, "We don't want to start a run on these." After pointing out that (between mine and Shirley's) they would only be giving out two additional awards, I finally received in the mail my own full-grown statuette. Since the Academy did not want the little one back, I now have two Oscars. Well, one and a half.

Bringing home an Academy Award did not change me, my life, or my career in any significant way. I placed the miniature gold statuette on a shelf, and life resumed as before for the Jarman family. My routine of school on the MGM lot and playing football with the neighborhood kids was not interrupted. Besides, I had already won an award from *Parents* magazine and several other honors for *The Yearling*. To me, the Oscar was just another trophy. Our family dynamic did not suffer because my sister Mildred was never envious of my success, and our parents never indulged in preferential "star treatment."

But my sudden Hollywood fame had triggered some changes, especially for my father. It may sound strange, but I never actually knew him until we moved to California. In Nashville, he was always either at work or exhausted from working seven days a week. When we spent summers with my grandparents, my father would stay behind and work, only visiting on occasional weekends. Now that he was around all the time as my guardian, I began to understand him for the first time. Claude Jarman Sr. was a quietly responsible, humble man who had struggled for years to gain a foothold in Nashville, only to have the rug pulled from under him as he was thrown into the challenging world of Hollywood. Yet I never once heard him complain. He felt comfortable with working-class folks—he socialized with the grips, the electricians, the film-industry employees without the glamorous jobs. His best friend was a studio policeman, Jim Moffett. We spent many evenings with him and his family.

My mother, on the other hand, carried a sense of entitlement her whole life. She had not only been born to a family of means—and had been the first female to attend the elite Webb School—but was also the prettiest girl in town. She married my father when she was twenty-three, and although she was a wonderful cook, played the piano beautifully, and was skilled in the arts of knitting and sewing, she never once worked outside the home. She never rode a bus or pumped a gallon of gasoline herself. In their ways, both my parents were products of a bygone era. Men worked hard, silent, and uncomplaining, and women stayed home and behaved in a ladylike manner. Neither of my parents ever "went Hollywood." Because of this, Mildred and I remained grounded and stable.

Meanwhile, MGM's massive publicity machine, headed by Howard Strickling, shifted into overdrive to promote its young Oscar-winner. For contract players, there were no talent agents or personal managers—the studio controlled everything. "We told stars what they could and couldn't say," Strickling once said, "and they did what we said because they knew we knew best." This about summed up the studio's attitude. Strickling was as old-school as they came: he started working for Metro Pictures Corporation in the silent days of 1919, before they merged into Metro-Goldwyn-Mayer. From 1934 until his retirement in 1969, he was head of the MGM publicity department and worked closely with "fixer" Eddie Mannix to ensure the public perceived the stars as perfect. When Clark Gable fathered Loretta Young's illegitimate baby in 1935, Strickling camouflaged the incident before the public caught a whiff of scandal. He also arranged for Van Johnson to marry the newly-divorced wife of his best friend, Keenan Wynn, to squash rumors of Van's homosexuality. Such was the power of the studio system.

As I had no scandals to cover up, I rarely worked directly with Strickling. My press man was Jack Atlas, a promotion expert who pioneered the medium of movie trailers. He arranged a steady flow of exclusive interviews and photo ops with the newspapers and movie magazines. *Photoplay, Screenland,* and *Motion Picture* were three of the biggest, but there were over a dozen movie-obsessed monthlies back in Hollywood's heyday, and Mr. Atlas made sure I appeared in all of them. In 1947, the *Motion Picture Herald* ranked me sixth in their yearly poll "The Top Ten Stars of Tomorrow," as voted by film distributors nationwide. Evelyn Keyes came in first place, with Elizabeth Taylor, Peter Lawford, and Angela Lansbury also recognized.

Hedda Hopper must have taken a liking to me. Though MGM worked closely with Hopper—offering her exclusive gossip in exchange for her build-up of its new stars—if she disliked someone, nothing could stop her poisoned pen from dripping venom. But she seemed genuinely fond of child actors. She mentioned my name in her weekly syndicated column at least once a month, reporting that I was going to be a household name, that producer Arthur Freed was "determined" to cast me as Huckleberry Finn in a musical version of the Twain classic, that I would star with Margaret O'Brien in *The Secret Garden,* that Lewis Milestone hoped to cast me in his adaptation of John Steinbeck's *The Red Pony,* and on and on. It was all lost on me; I never read a word of her column or the fan magazines. I just showed up for the interviews.

I not only had my own publicity man but my own wardrobe person, as well as hair and makeup specialists to keep every hair in place for the photos and public appearances. This was the full MGM treatment as orchestrated by Louis B. Mayer himself.

All the movie stars worked regularly on radio too. Gregory Peck, Jane Wyman, and I performed *The Yearling* twice on the air for Lux Radio Theatre and Screen Actors Guild Playhouse. We had a live audience, and I had to authentically cry in all the key emotional scenes, just as I had for the camera—only this time I had no deer, no location or props, and no Clarence to coax the tears. Somehow I managed to weep in all the right places. I still have a 78 record of one of those *Yearling* performances. At Christmas, I went to New York and acted in another radio drama called *The Day They Gave Babies Away.* After we finished the live program, I found out I had to repeat the whole performance over again for the West Coast! I was still learning the hard way.

When the applause died down and all the flashbulbs had gone off, my father and I would return home every evening to our modest Culver City bungalow. Unless I was required at some night-time industry function or film premiere, I would have a quiet dinner with my family and sleep on the rollaway bed in the living room. I didn't even have my own bedroom. I was practically leading a double life.

Metro-Goldwyn-Mayer did make *The Red Pony*, but not with me. Lewis Milestone, the Oscar-winning director of *All Quiet on the Western Front,* had always envisioned me as Tom, the boy who is given the pony. I even had several conversations with the film's star, Robert Mitchum, in which he assured me, "You're shoe-in." But no one was prepared for my growth spurt. After shooting my first two movies, I sprouted up faster than the baby deer in *The Yearling.* By 1947, I was six inches taller and, though I was only twelve, was suddenly too big to believably portray a little kid on-screen. This created a casting conundrum. I had the face and voice of a child, but I towered over other children—and some of the adults too. MGM's solution? Loan the kid out for a Western.

Studios often loaned their contract stars out to competing studios for a profit, either as punishment for bad behavior or, in my case, because their home studio had no roles appropriate for them at the time. RKO paid MGM $50,000 for my services on a picture called *Roughshod.* I was only being paid $250 per week at that time, but I wasn't complaining. I did receive a $10,000 bonus after the film was completed, and I had a thoroughly enjoyable experience making it. Plus, I learned a lot about horses. And even a little about women.

Robert Sterling, the son of silent-era Western star William S. Hart, played a cowboy named Clay, and I was his younger brother, Steve. It was a fairly juicy and atypical role for a child. It gave me a chance to shine as the good guy who, in some respects, is wiser and more sophisticated than his grown brother. In the film, I try to persuade Clay to marry a dance-hall girl (Gloria Grahame) because I believe she is a good person.

For film historians, *Roughshod* is noteworthy as one of director Mark Robson's early films. Robson went on to direct Kirk Douglas in *Champion,* William Holden and Grace Kelly in *The Bridges at Toko-Ri,* Frank Sinatra in *Von Ryan's Express,* and a host of other stars in acclaimed classics. For me, a boy of twelve going on thirteen, *Roughshod* was a rare opportunity to live in a tent for twelve weeks on location in the majestic High Sierras and ride horses every day. It was like a three-month camping excursion. The cast and crew slept in sturdy, comfortable tents beneath the stars and ate our meals together in another large tent. I lived right there with the horse wranglers, who took me on all-day rides in the hills and taught me all they knew about riding. We didn't just ride horses in the picture; we rode them off-camera to our next filming location instead of packing them into a trailer. I became an expert young horseman.

The women in the picture, however, proved too much for me to wrangle. Blonde RKO vixen Gloria Grahame was the leader of a group of lovely saloon girls played by Myrna Dell, Martha Hyer, and Jeff Donnell. With her reputation, one might expect Gloria to be sexually assertive with the boys. While married to director Nicholas Ray, she reportedly began a relationship with her thirteen-year-old stepson! But in fact, Gloria was just a nice lady to me—sweet and a bit motherly. It was twenty-three-year-old platinum knockout Myrna Dell I had to watch out for. Myrna was quite a piece of work. "Come here, I'll teach you how to kiss, boy!" she would beckon whenever she got the chance, a seductive smile on her face and a wink in her eye. I wasn't sure how serious she was, but she was ten years older and a little too advanced for me.

But I adored all the ladies in the film and would have signed up for a sequel in a heartbeat.

I did experience my first kiss while shooting *Roughshod,* but it was not with Myrna. I managed to find a girl my own age. Joan Ruman, the daughter of our production manager Sam Ruman, was out of school for the summer and visiting her dad on location. Our base camp was just outside of Bridgeport, California, best known to film noir fans as the setting for *Out of the Past,* starring icon-of-cool Robert Mitchum. In fact, RKO had sent Mitchum, along with director Jacques Tourneur and crew, to shoot in Bridgeport six months before we arrived. There was not much to do in the rural area besides ride horses. Joan and I spent evenings together attending rodeos, taking walks or horse rides, and just talking. It was a casual summer romance that kick-started my growing interest in the opposite sex.

When I returned to Los Angeles in August of 1947, I don't think I ever saw Joan again, but I did start going on dates with girls. Paddy Costello—daughter of Lou Costello, half of the Abbott and Costello comedy duo—called and invited me to her thirteenth birthday party, and we talked on the phone frequently. I also went out occasionally with a girl named Geraldine who had been an extra in one of the town scenes in *The Yearling.*

I was the pet of the RKO Radio *"Roughshod"*
Company and sometimes the girls succeeded in running me
down. Being only thirteen, I much preferred the company
of the men on the show. Here I have been captured by
Gloria Grahame (R), Myrna Dell and Jeff Donnell (L).

It was about this time that I crossed paths with another young performer who was just starting a picture at RKO as I was wrapping mine up. Her family called her Natasha, but she was known professionally as Natalie Wood. When I first saw her, she was sitting in a little classroom on the RKO lot studying all by herself, her hair tightly braided in pigtails. She was on loan-out for *The Green Promise* from her home studio, Fox. She was a few years younger than I was and a very sweet kid. Later I went out on a date or two with her when I came back to Hollywood after high school graduation, and she was doing TV work. That was the early 1950s, and she was just about to break through with her Oscar-nominated role in *Rebel Without a Cause,* a landmark teen drama that would send her fame into orbit. Unlike me, Natalie was in the Hollywood game for the long haul.

For some mysterious reason, RKO did not release *Roughshod* for two years, shelving it until 1949. Even today, the film is not widely shown. Those who have seen it categorize it as an intriguing blend of Western and film noir.

Of course, RKO would someday become synonymous with noir, but at the time, no one knew that. There was a simmering undercurrent of gritty realism and moody lighting—often born out of budgetary restrictions—that only appears to be a movement or a film genre in retrospect. If you had asked me then, I might have predicted that Gloria Grahame would earn a special place in film history, though I didn't know RKO had just bought her, lock stock and barrel, from Metro. *Roughshod* was the first picture RKO made with her under contract. I might also have predicted that Mark Robson would be a big-name director. I was unaware of his work with producer Val Lewton, but Robson crafted every scene in *Roughshod* with the dedication of a master. Like Clarence Brown, he nurtured my performance rather than rushing it and had a hands-on way of ensuring each shot was just the way he envisioned it.

Clarence, meanwhile, had wrapped his production of *Song of Love* with Katharine Hepburn and was gearing up to produce *The Secret Garden*. The first sound-era adaptation of Frances Hodgson Burnett's beloved novel would star my recess playmate Margaret O'Brien and my classmate Dean Stockwell in the role Clarence had wanted me for. "We're going in a different direction," he told me, which was the standard Hollywood line for "We decided not to cast you." But I wasn't crying. It turns out that Clarence had me in mind for a part that would be even better.

CHAPTER 5

Hollywood Comes to
Faulkner's Home

I f I had to choose one word to describe Hollywood in the summer
of 1948, it would be euphoric.

The heady postwar years had officially arrived. Theaters
were reporting huge box-office returns, and the quality of motion
pictures had never been surpassed. All of Los Angeles seemed to be
celebrating. On any given night, you might spot Rita Hayworth,
Frank Sinatra, and Errol Flynn stepping out at Ciro's. Betty Grable,
Humphrey Bogart, Joan Crawford, or Cary Grant might be seen dining at Romanoff's. Everyone glittered in their finest attire. Though I
was too young to indulge in the nightlife, we all shared in the com-
mon feeling of optimistic revelry; it was thick in the air.

Movies were good and getting better all the time. Warner Bros.
was just releasing John Huston's *Key Largo* with Bogart and Bacall, as
well as Doris Day's first film, *Romance on the High Seas*. United Artists
was planning the premiere of Howard Hawks's *Red River,* a John
Wayne Western featuring Montgomery Clift in his film debut. At
Paramount, Billy Wilder and Charles Brackett were writing the script
for *Sunset Boulevard,* now considered to be one of the greatest movies

Hollywood ever produced. Writer Mary Orr was busy adapting her story "The Wisdom of Eve" into a play that Twentieth Century Fox would turn into *All About Eve,* yet another of the most acclaimed films in history. A supporting role in *All About Eve* would be given to a new actress Fox was grooming for stardom named Marilyn Monroe.

Down in Culver City, MGM was leading the pack and was at the top of their game. On Stage 30, Esther Williams could be found splashing in the ninety-foot swimming pool they had built for her. Bombshell Lana Turner reigned as the unofficial queen of the lot. She had recently starred in *Homecoming* with "The King," Clark Gable, who was making pictures again after a three-year stint with the air force. Ad campaigns for *Adventure,* costarring Gable and Greer Garson, had featured the tagline "Gable's back and Garson's got him!" The movie didn't live up to the hype, but that line was the studio's proud boast that their king had returned and all was right with the world. That summer, Metro was reaping profits from the current top box-office attraction in the country, *Easter Parade* with Judy Garland and Fred Astaire. In the cutting room, they were editing *The Three Musketeers,* a Technicolor adventure that would become the highest-grossing Hollywood film of 1948.

Ironically, at this golden apex of moviemaking, I was shunted into my first flop. Hoping to recapture the magic of *The Yearling,* MGM purchased the rights to another Marjorie Kinnan Rawlings story called "A Family for Jock," a heartwarming tale about a grieving opera singer, an orphaned boy, and a heroic dog. Renaming it "Mountain Prelude," the studio had it published in the *Saturday Evening Post* before transforming it into a screen vehicle for their beloved canine star, Lassie. Renamed yet again *The Sun in the Morning,* then finally *The Sun Comes Up,* it became MGM's fifth in a series of seven Lassie movies.

Roddy McDowall and Elizabeth Taylor (in her first major role) had set a high standard with the 1943 original, *Lassie Come Home.* The simple, sincere story of a boy's bond with his dog won over audiences, turned a handsome profit, and is still regarded as a family classic today. In fact, that film kick-started a pop-culture phenomenon and a worldwide collie craze. With each subsequent entry in the series, though, the studio seemed to skimp more and more on quality. By the time they got to number five, Lassie had been relegated to B-picture status. *The Sun Comes Up* was a pale rehash of the same old formula, only this time the dog had two new costars: me and former soprano superstar Jeanette MacDonald.

Personally, I wasn't a particular fan of the Lassie movies. I had no great desire to act with the famous collie, but the MGM powers that be decreed this would be my next assignment, and I had no choice but to comply. At least I had a natural affinity for animals, and I figured a trained dog would be easier to work with than a deer. I would also have the pleasure of working with a group of delightful supporting players: solid character actor Lloyd Nolan, Pa Kettle himself Percy Kilbride, and Margaret Hamilton, best known as the one and only Wicked Witch of the West.

According to the theatrical trailer, *The Sun Comes Up* was chock-full of "the kind of drama that made *The Yearling* great." But without Clarence Brown's expert direction or a decent budget, it was a poor man's *Yearling*. From the beginning, I could tell I was in for a letdown from the type of filmmaking experience I was used to. My first clue was the location. We shot it in Santa Cruz, California, which was somehow expected to pass for North Carolina's Blue Ridge Mountain range and a slow Southern town called Brushy Gap. My next clue was the director, Richard Thorpe, known primarily as a workman who could deliver the product on time and under budget. After helming over 100 cheaply-produced silents and early talkies—including a string of B-Westerns with titles like *Fast Fightin'*, *Rough Ridin'*, and *Tearin' into Trouble*—Mr. Thorpe had worked his way up to somewhat glossier material by the 1940s. His bread-and-butter was the formula picture—*Tarzan*, *Lassie*, Esther Williams, even a *Thin Man* sequel. He was quick and efficient, with no artistic aspirations to get in the way.

Then there was the makeup. In the movie, I develop pneumonia and am nursed back to health by a writer, played by Lloyd Nolan. Apparently, one summer when he was young and struggling, Lloyd got a deep tan on the beach at Cape Cod. When he was cast as a pirate in a Broadway show, he credited his big break to his suntanned face and his golden brown skin became something of a trademark. To my dismay, the makeup artists on the film tried to match my fair skin to Lloyd's by packing a thick layer of dark pancake foundation on my face daily. I had never worn makeup before! Clarence had shunned it in *The Yearling*—even Jayne Wyman appeared bare-faced. Now I felt self-conscious and ridiculous.

Everyone got along fine, but none of the cast seemed especially enthusiastic about the project. I don't know which of my costars was more disgruntled—Lassie or Jeanette MacDonald. Jeanette had been one of MGM's top stars in the late 1930s. Often paired in fanciful musicals with baritone Nelson Eddy, she sang operatic songs in a string of hit movies until World War II shifted public tastes. In 1943, her contract was not renewed. After five years away from the screen, she returned to Metro in 1948 for the comeback vehicle *Three Daring Daughters*. It failed to generate much buzz, and Jeanette, like me, found herself stuck in a Lassie movie. It would be her final film.

with Lloyd Nolan, Jeanette MacDonald
and Lassie on the set of *"The Sun Comes Up"*

I could understand her frustration. Every morning, makeup man Lee Stanfield would attach extra tufts of fur to the dog's nether-regions to disguise the fact that Lassie was really a male dog named Pal. He would then head over to Jeanette's trailer to apply her makeup. One day, Jeanette asked Lee directly if he made up Lassie first. "Yes, I do," he admitted. "From now on," she told him, "I think we ought to reverse that." This woman, who had been pampered like a diva for years, was now second in line to a trained collie. She smiled and did her best, but dissatisfaction seeped through the cracks in her professional exterior.

Even Pal, our celebrated Lassie himself, seemed none too thrilled to be there. Perhaps old age was setting in, or maybe the years of performing as a female impersonator were starting to take their toll. One day we shot a touching scene where I shared a heart-to-heart moment with Lassie. I was supposed to reach under his muzzle and gently cradle his chin in my palm as I spoke my line. It worked fine in rehearsal, but when the cameras rolled, I placed my hand under Pal's chin and, without warning, he opened his jaws and clamped them down right on the side of my face.

"Cut!" Mr. Thorpe shouted.

"Oh my god!" a woman screamed.

I could hear the panicked gasps as a dozen feet scuffled around me. Director, crew members, dog wrangler, and the on-set nurse rushed over to assess the damage. Blood gushed from the wound on my cheek, and I was a bit dazed. What just happened? Had America's favorite dog really bitten me in the face?

Brushing Lassie before he bit me on the cheek in 1949

Luckily, the damage was not severe. Rubbing alcohol was swabbed over the gash, and I was sent home to recover. The next morning, I reported to the set at the usual time. An even thicker layer of tan pancake makeup was applied over the teeth marks, and we continued shooting the scene right where we had left off. The show must go on. But privately I wondered how, after the worldwide acclaim *The Yearling* had received less than two years earlier, I could have been relegated to such an inferior film. I had been discovered and nurtured by the best in the business. Now, without a strong director, I was left floundering to deliver the best performance I knew how. I could tell my work was acceptable but far from inspired.

Reviewers collectively yawned at yet another Lassie picture. Edwin Schallert of the *Los Angeles Times* noted that Jeanette MacDonald and I performed our roles competently, though he observed that I was too tall to play a child. One critic wrote, "Even Lassie was bad." For a young composer named Andre Previn, *The Sun Comes Up* was a memorable experience—it was his first feature film score. From working on a Lassie movie, Previn would go on to become one of the most lauded conductors and composers in history and would marry actress Mia Farrow in 1970. I, however, could not wait to forget Lassie and move on to my next project.

William Faulkner was one of America's great twentieth-century authors and part of the glorious Hollywood studio system. He spent years honing his craft in Culver City and Burbank, collaborating on scripts for Howard Hawks, Jean Renoir, and other auteurs of the era. Back then, movie studios literally combed the world for talent. This method worked brilliantly. (It certainly worked for me!) The top studios dispatched scouts to Midwestern and Eastern cities and even across to Europe to hunt down the planet's best actors, writers, directors, cinematographers, and editors. If they could round up a stockpile of geniuses, they figured, their organization would create the greatest pictures and win the most awards. The goal was not just to rake in money but to be the best studio in town.

With William Faulkner on the set of
"Intruder in the Dust" 1949

MGM had first paid for Faulkner to come west in 1932. He was an acclaimed but impoverished and fairly obscure writer with six novels to his name, most of which sold poorly. Talkies had created a need for clever dialogue when they took over in 1929. Some of the most gifted wordsmiths of the era—including F. Scott Fitzgerald, John Steinbeck, and Aldous Huxley—were hired to sit in cramped offices on studio lots and crank out screenplays. Faulkner bounced between writing novels at his home in Oxford, Mississippi, and writing scripts in Los Angeles from 1932 until the late 1940s, when he won the Nobel Prize for literature and finally achieved widespread recognition.

In 1948, at the tail end of his Hollywood years, Faulkner penned a short novel inspired by racial tensions in the South. It was the very early days of the civil rights movement, when Harry Truman signed an executive order desegregating the armed forces and tried to pass an anti-lynching measure that was opposed by many Southern states. *Intruder in the Dust* was an understated yet powerful story about two teenage boys—one black and one white—and an elderly woman who help a lawyer prove the innocence of an African-American man wrongly accused of murder. Set in a small Southern town, Faulkner's *Intruder* was something of a precursor to Harper Lee's 1960 classic *To Kill a Mockingbird.*

Clarence Brown was immediately interested in turning the novel into a film, and he convinced Louis B. Mayer and new head of production Dore Schary to purchase the screen rights. Coercing MGM to actually shoot the film was another matter. Though he and Clarence were close friends, Mayer would probably never have allowed it. But Schary was a risk-taker with a keen social conscience, and he green-lit the "message picture" (as they called them then), though messages against racism were virtually nonexistent in 1940s Hollywood. Films like this simply weren't being made yet. MGM took a chance on being the first of the "big five" studios to tackle a project about white folks learning to respect the rights of a black man. It may seem like a primitive step today, but in a time when racist attitudes were prevalent, making a movie of *Intruder in the Dust* was akin to taking a first step on the moon.

From the beginning, Clarence knew I would play the lead role of Chick Mallison. He originally planned to reunite "Jody" and "Pa" by casting Gregory Peck as Chick's uncle John, the lawyer. Greg apparently loved the story but felt the part was too minor for him at that point in his career. In the two years since completing *The Yearling*, Gregory Peck had risen to the heights of stardom with Best Picture Oscar-winner *Gentleman's Agreement* and Alfred Hitchcock's *The Paradine Case*. He was just signing on to deliver an iconic performance as General Frank Savage in *Twelve O'Clock High* when he turned down Clarence's offer. If Greg had appeared in *Intruder in the Dust*, it might have received more attention—but who could blame him? With the help of Darryl F. Zanuck, he was forging his own distinct path to screen immortality. The part of the lawyer instead went to David Brian, an actor who came to Clarence's attention through Joan Crawford, who had discovered him. I thought he was excellent in the role.

Intruder in the Dust was a joy to make. The hardships and challenges of *The Yearling* seemed light years away as I got to know a very different Clarence Brown—one who was warm, trusting, and confident in my abilities.

Just prior to shooting, my grandmother died, and her funeral in Tennessee delayed my arrival to the set. When my dad and I arrived at our location—Faulkner's hometown of Oxford, Mississippi—we were greeted with open arms. This was Faulkner country, and only about 240 miles from the town where I had been born. I felt right at home there.

It still amazes me how welcoming the town was, considering the fact that we were making an anti-lynching film that exposed deeply embedded racism in the South. These were the days of segregation; the African-American actors in the cast stayed in local homes while the Caucasians were given hotel accommodations. Aside from this glaring injustice, I never witnessed any bias from the locals. Oxford rolled out the red carpet to black and white alike, thrilled that Hollywood had descended upon their community.

With David Brian, *"Intruder in the Dust"*, in 1949

Our melting pot of a cast melted right into the town. Young African-American actor Elzie Emanuel played my partner-in-crime Aleck, and we spent time together off-screen too. Someone in Oxford was always throwing a party or a catfish-fry, and we made the rounds. A restaurant in the town square had a jukebox, and when we weren't filming, I could be found there dropping dimes into the slot. "Ghost Riders in the Sky" by Stan Jones and the Death Valley Rangers was my favorite record. I played it so often that my father said he'd like to "strangle the guy that wrote that song." Dad was not a fan.

The town square served as a major setting for the film, with local men, women, and children of all races gathered around the courthouse for the crowd scenes. All the extra and bit parts were played by citizens of Oxford. Those not employed as extras would stand outside of camera range and watch quietly. I got the impression that our movie brought out the best in the townspeople. It seemed to generate a feeling of camaraderie and community pride. For our part, the "intruders" from Hollywood felt we were doing something important, in our small way, to address long-held prejudices and perhaps even change a few minds. We were as proud to be there as Oxford was to have us.

Our entire cast was incredible. Elizabeth Patterson, who played the stalwart Miss Habersham, had been born in Tennessee in 1874. She would find television immortality at age seventy-seven playing Lucy's neighbor Mrs. Trumbull on *I Love Lucy*. Porter Hall was instantly recognizable from movies like *The Thin Man, His Girl Friday*, and *Double Indemnity*. His heartbreaking performance as Nub Gowrie is among the finest in his long career. Will Geer's flawless portrayal of Sheriff Hampton had us all convinced he was a good ol' country boy, until we filmed the scene where the Sheriff drives Lucas up to the jail. Will kept asking Clarence, "Can I practice driving the car before we shoot?" We soon found out he was a New York City stage actor who had never driven a car before. For his and everyone else's safety, a stunt driver was used.

The gifted Juano Hernandez, a Puerto Rican, was entrusted with the film's most difficult characterization, Lucas Beauchamp, the falsely accused black man whose only crime is pride. Faulkner himself helped to coach Hernandez in speaking like an uneducated Southerner. Reciting Shakespeare came more naturally to him than dropping his G's, but he rose to the challenge of Lucas brilliantly.

William Faulkner had given Clarence's adaptation his blessing, and he visited the set a couple of times a week. He was still under contract to Warner Bros. at that time, so he was technically prohibited from working on the film. That didn't stop him from doing a few gratis revisions on the script now and then; Clarence would often ask him to rewrite a piece of screenwriter Ben Maddow's dialogue, and he was happy to oblige. He struck me as pleased that someone in Hollywood understood and appreciated his novel enough to try and do it justice cinematically. Like Clarence, William Faulkner was driven by a quiet, thoughtful kind of intelligence. But Faulkner never felt at home in Hollywood, even though he worked there off and on for fifteen years. He always claimed he knew little about the medium. After attending the premiere of *Intruder,* he humbly stated, "I don't know much about movies, but I thought it was one of the best I've ever seen."

With Juano Hernandez, *"Intruder in the Dust",* 1949

We gathered at Faulkner's house many weekends. His pretty blonde daughter, Jill, was around my age. She and her mother, Estelle, were friendly and easy to talk to. Like everyone else in Oxford, the Faulkners opened their doors with Southern hospitality. Mr. Faulkner even let me ride his own beloved horse, Highboy, in the movie. I'm not sure if I was aware of his well-publicized alcoholism at that time, but Faulkner was a gentleman who never let his composure slip in front of others. In fact, he was so circumspect in his communication, I don't think we ever exchanged more than the basic pleasantries of "Hello" and "How are you?" He was not much for small talk. Apparently, he saved his words for the written page.

By the time our small crew left Oxford in late April of 1949, Twentieth Century Fox and United Artists each had a "message picture" in production, both addressing racism in America. But I felt gratified knowing that we broached that territory before it was a trend. To this day, I am honored to be a part of *Intruder in the Dust*. Clarence wove techniques of film noir, silent cinema, and Italy's new style of neorealism together into a quietly powerful mystery that perfectly encapsulated a time and place in American history. Frustrations over racial injustice were beginning to simmer in Mississippi, but it would be over a decade before they boiled over. When college student James Meredith became the first African-American to attend Ole Miss in 1962, two men were killed in riots that erupted right there in Oxford. If we had tried to film *Intruder* ten years later, it would have been impossible. But at that moment it time, in the early spring of 1949, it all came together.

MGM had the guts to let Clarence produce and direct the film, but they faltered on the follow-through. Mayer and Schary must have gotten nervous about the controversial theme because they seemed to bury *Intruder in the Dust*. Critics loved it, and *Life* ran a three-page spread, but the studio's advertising and distribution were weak. It would be interesting to examine old exhibitor records and determine if the studio even distributed the movie across the Southern states. I doubt it.

Because Clarence shot the film without sound, we had to loop every bit of our dialogue once we got back to Culver City, delaying the release. *Intruder* wound up being lost in the shuffle of other early racial-themed dramas like the independently-funded *Lost Boundaries,* UA's *Home of the Brave,* and Fox's Oscar-nominated *Pinky,* all released before our film.

Intruder won no Oscars, but it did win a BAFTA (British Academy Award), and Golden Globe nominations for David Brian as Best Supporting Actor and for Juano Hernandez as Most Promising Newcomer of 1950. His performance, and the entire film, was far better appreciated in Europe. Outside of the United States, it was seen as impressive to present a new type of African-American character on the screen—dignified and defiant, refusing to kowtow to white men. Within postwar America, it was seen as subversive and unsettling. Still, *Intruder* gave Hernandez his first major role, launching his Hollywood career. He would be active in film and television through the 1960s. He died in 1970.

The scene between Juano and me, where Chick visits Lucas in the jail cell, remains my favorite. My light hands clasp the bars next to his dark hands, but instead of seeing a contrast of black and white, we notice how similar they are. Dappled with shadows and varying shades of gray, our hands form equal parts of an intricate pattern. With the help of Robert Surtees's camera, Clarence used his silent-movie skills and a bit of noir lighting to create a beautiful shot that, to me, is the heart and soul of the film.

No faces are seen, just our hands on the bars as Chick asks Lucas, "Why me? What can I do about it?"

"You ain't cluttered," Lucas says. "You can listen, but adults are too full of notions."

Without preaching or using a heavy-handed approach, the scene suggests that harmony between the races might be possible if men were willing to reevaluate their old notions.

New York Times critic Bosley Crowther called *Intruder in the Dust* "this year's preeminent picture and one of the great cinema dramas of our times." The *Times* published his review along with a separate article proclaiming the film's importance as a social commentary. It "cuts closer to the core of the fundamental nature of racism in the South than any film we've yet had," Crowther wrote.

The cast and direction were unanimously praised, and I received my best notices since *The Yearling*. "Claude Jarman lays bare the seething, complex emotional structure of a growing boy," wrote *Modern Screen*. Sadly, the film was largely overlooked and quickly forgotten.

In 1968, critic Pauline Kael devoted three pages to discussing *Intruder in the Dust* in her book *Kiss Kiss Bang Bang*. A passionate and highly opinionated reviewer, Kael reassessed the film at a critical time in civil rights history: Martin Luther King Jr. had just been assassinated and President Johnson had signed the Fair Housing Act. She championed *Intruder*, pondering what-if scenarios that would have made the film better appreciated. "If this movie had been produced in Europe, it would probably be widely acclaimed . . . Had [it] been directed by a young unknown, it might have been called a masterpiece." Her words were thought-provoking but didn't spark much of a revival—the film was out of print and would not be released to the public for decades.

The twenty-first century has brought a new appreciation for *Intruder in the Dust*. It can now be easily viewed online or on disc. In 2010, when the film turned sixty, I went back to Oxford and reunited with many of the bit players who still lived in town. My wife and I toured Rowan Oak, the Faulkner home, which is now a museum. The outpouring of love warmed my heart; the community embraced this groundbreaking drama as great entertainment and a key moment in the history of Mississippi. The film noir world has also embraced *Intruder* with popular screenings at Noir City in San Francisco and Arthur Lyons Film Noir Festival in Palm Springs. Professor Albert Johnson, a senior lecturer in the African American Studies Department at the University of California, Berkeley, used to travel the world discussing race relations in American cinema, and *Intruder in the Dust* was the film he always showed in his presentation.

In 1950, a year after making the movie, I ran into William Faulkner on a layover at the Memphis airport. "Mr. Faulkner," I said, "how are you?"

"Fine," he replied.

"How's Oxford?"

"Fine."

"Well, it's been nice talking to you, Mr. Faulkner."

That was the last time I saw him. Nine years later, he was badly injured while riding his horse and died shortly thereafter.

Faulkner created the original story, and MGM allowed it to be made, but *Intruder in the Dust* exists solely because of one man: Clarence Brown. When I think back on my time in Hollywood, I realize what a profound influence he had on my life. Not only because he had discovered me in that classroom back in Nashville. Not only because he singlehandedly cast me, guided and nurtured me through my first film. His outlook—his thoroughness and unwavering devotion to his craft—affected my life on some level. I could never be as meticulous as Clarence, but I was inspired to try, as he did, to focus on every little detail of anything that was important to me. He was so detail-oriented, I would have trusted him with my life. An avid pilot, he used to take me flying over Santa Monica in his tiny little single-engine plane. I was never scared for a minute.

He inspired me to put work first. He was wise enough to know the end product is what counts; the films are what remain long after the filmmakers and stars have died. Clarence did not suffer fools, nor was he interested in pandering to the press or attention-seeking. He avoided the flashy, scandalous side of Hollywood life, which is probably why no book about Clarence Brown has ever been published. Near the end of his life, I paid him a visit at his home in Indian Wells, in the California desert. I asked, "Why don't you write a book?" He replied, "No one would be interested unless I told dirty little secrets." Simple as that.

What a phenomenal career Clarence had. He directed fifty-two motion pictures—one for every card in a deck. His films earned a total of nine Academy Awards and thirty-eight nominations. Clarence was nominated for Best Director six times but never won. He directed the legendary Greta Garbo in seven of her greatest films; he was her favorite director. He and his wife Marian used to travel through Europe with Garbo. They dined together often, but when the check came, he told me, "She never once offered to pay it." She carried her sense of entitlement like a crown.

As fond as he was of Garbo, Joan Crawford was number one with Clarence. He directed her in six of her early films as she steadily rose to stardom. Joan adored Clarence. He told me she even propositioned him, saying, "Remember, Clarence, it's always there if you want it." I don't know if he ever took her up on her offer, but he would get a certain look in his eye when he talked about Joan. He'd say, "What a dame!" Those three words said it all. Clarence was married four times, but his last marriage to Marian Spies lasted forty years. As he explained to me, "It took a few tries to get it right."

Between his talent, his work ethic, and his willingness to spend ample time to get a shot perfect, Clarence raised the standard of the entire industry. He was an expert camera technician with an engineering degree from the University of Tennessee. He claimed he invented the over-the-shoulder shot, and he probably did. He was one of the original creative motion-picture pioneers.

In 1970, Clarence funded the Clarence Brown Theatre for the Performing Arts at the University of Tennessee. Jane Wyman and I attended the opening ceremony, where we screened a print of *The Yearling.* I saw him several more times before he died in 1987, at the age of ninety-seven.

Though he directed four more films before officially retiring in 1952, *Intruder in the Dust* was truly Clarence Brown's swan song. This was a film he had longed to make, and he made it his own way. Whether it succeeded or failed with the public didn't seem to faze him. He had accomplished what he set out to accomplish, and that was enough for him.

CHAPTER 6

"I Ain't Scared"

Metro-Goldwyn-Mayer Studios, Inc. was born when exhibitor Marcus Loew merged Metro Pictures, Goldwyn Pictures, and Louis B. Mayer Pictures on April 17, 1924. The studio was an instant success, growing more profitable with each year. It was the last major studio to convert to sound pictures, yet it remained the most successful of all film studios during the Great Depression. April of 1949 marked MGM's first major milestone: its twenty-fifth anniversary.

I had returned to the studio from Mississippi just in time for the big Silver Jubilee celebration luncheon. I was settling back into the routine of Culver City, the little two-room schoolhouse, and my continuing drama lessons with Lillian Burns. Like every single contract player on the roster, I was ordered to be present at noon for the luncheon. One of the soundstages was all decked out with banquet tables and an elevated stage where the stars were introduced, one by one, by longtime MGM actor (and Screen Actors Guild president) George Murphy. Staff members, exhibitors, and executives filled the hall, with the contract players seated up on the stage facing an audience as we ate! This was a lunchbreak, Hollywood style. We were served chicken and expected to enjoy it while a movie camera panned over the brightly-lit face of every actor, neatly arranged in alphabetical order and grinning for the camera. My face was not exactly smiling, but then I sat next to Buster Keaton, whose deadpan humor had grown more understated through the years until he barely had a word to say.

Watching the footage is a trip back in time. I notice how busy everyone was. Movies were hard work: six days a week, often twelve or more hours a day. Several stars—Janet Leigh, Jennifer Jones, and Mario Lanza, to name a few—rushed in from their sets fully costumed. They ate, smoked a cigarette, and rushed right back to work. I can almost feel the high-energy bustle that gripped the lot in those days.

Many of us frequently ate lunch in the commissary together, but this was the first time the whole gang gathered together in one room. Of course, as a kid actor, I fraternized little with the adult stars. I thought Jimmy Durante was especially nice and funny, and a little later, Debbie Reynolds joined MGM. Our paths only crossed briefly—I was on my way out as she was on her way in—but running into her was a bright spot in my day. She was only two years older than I and always warm and friendly.

Surprisingly, the adult MGM star who treated me the most like a friend was none other than Frank Sinatra himself. Equally beloved and feared, incredibly generous and notoriously vindictive, Sinatra was a one-of-a-kind guy. Tommy Dorsey was once quoted as saying about Frank: "He's the most fascinating man in the world, but don't stick your hand in the cage." I never saw Frank snap; I only witnessed his kind and courteous side. He always greeted me with a broad smile and a handshake and seemed genuinely glad to see me. Once, when I came back to the MGM lot while on leave from the Navy in 1958, I walked on to the closed set where Frank, Dean Martin, and Shirley MacLaine were filming *Some Came Running*. The assistant director discreetly stopped me at the door. "You'd better leave," he whispered. "We're not sure how Mr. Sinatra might react to an unexpected visitor."

Just then, Frank emerged from his dressing room. He recognized me instantly and made a beeline to greet me with a welcoming

"Hello there!" and "How've you been?" We stood there and caught up for several minutes while everyone on the set, including director Vincente Minnelli, waited to continue shooting. Frank didn't care. He may have been difficult to work with, but everything he did, whether it was music or movies, he did as if he were in charge. And if he liked you, you knew it was straight from the heart. I would have loved to make a movie with him, but it was not to be.

My next assignment was yet another Western shot on location, this time in Kanab, Utah, a picturesque little village perched on top of the Grand Canyon just north of the Arizona border. The picture was *The Outriders,* and—though I didn't know it then—it would be my last contract film at MGM.

Westerns were entering a golden age. They had been wildly popular and cheap to make in the 1920s. When sound came along, the genre slid into a decline until the 1940s, when progressive directors like John Ford and advancements in color film technology kicked off a revival of high-quality Westerns. In the 1950s, there would be more Westerns made than any other type of film. I would make five of them. Once *Roughshod* was released in the summer of 1949, Western producers and directors saw that I could handle horses and was comfortable with Old West dialogue. My slight Tennessee twang added to the illusion that I was a natural-born cowboy.

In *The Outriders,* I was fourth-billed in a cast that included Western king Joel McCrea, Metro's latest Technicolor beauty Arlene Dahl, movie staple Barry Sullivan, and former superstar Ramon Novarro. In the silent days, Ramon had been MGM's golden boy. He was the star of their first enormous hit, the 1925 epic *Ben-Hur,* and one of the first Mexican-Americans to make it big in Hollywood. In his youth, Ramon played romantic lead to Greta Garbo, Norma Shearer, and Joan Crawford. He had recently returned to films after a decade away and was now playing character parts. Everyone on set was buzzing about his legendary career and comeback.

The lead was originally supposed to be Robert Taylor, but Joel McCrea somehow landed the role. Joel was not an MGM star; he had worked at a variety of studios, mostly RKO and Paramount, playing handsome leading men in 1930s and '40s comedies and a few dramas. But he claimed he always felt more comfortable in Westerns. "The minute I got a horse and a hat and a pair of boots on, I felt easier," McCrea once said. To me, he looked like a born horseman. I liked Joel but had virtually no dialogue with him. In fact, I barely interacted with any of the cast. I was practically making a cameo appearance.

Though I was given costar billing in *The Outriders,* this was not reflected in my character or my screen time. At 14, I played Roy, Arlene Dahl's young brother-in-law who travels with her in a wagon train across the West to Ohio. I appear nearly thirty minutes into the film and spend a grand total of about seven minutes on camera. Roy stubbornly tries to prove he's a man by continually saying, "I ain't scared," which is the extent of my character development before I die while foolishly attempting to cross a flooded river on horseback. It's unclear exactly why I decided to cross the river, as I didn't even get a close-up or any dialogue before I start across. In fact, it was such a distant long shot, I'm not sure audiences even realized it was my character that drowned! I thought working with Lassie was bad, but *The Outriders* was a new low.

There was little for me to do in the film, and off-screen there was even less to do in such a desolate location. Because we shot in the summer, there was no school, so I enjoyed having some rare downtime near the scenic Paria River. Sometimes I hung around with a handful of local teenagers. It was my first contact with disciples of the Mormon Church, an organization that seemed to pull the strings of everyone in Kanab. All the kids were eerily clean-cut and pious. I met girls my age who were getting married while still in high school. It was a whole different kind of lifestyle—one that made me feel isolated and a little depressed. There was no one around I could relate to except my dad.

One night, a bunch of crew members decided it would be fun to take my father to a bar and get him good and drunk. This was a first for my dad, as far as I knew. I had never seen him take a drink of anything stronger than eggnog at Christmas. I thought he was hilarious, stumbling in that night, but when he got violently sick and had a terrible hangover the following morning, I felt a little guilty for laughing. This was my dad's one stab at the wild Hollywood lifestyle, and it did not suit him. He never got drunk again.

I wrapped the film just in time to make the *Intruder in the Dust* opening in Nashville.

Though I had been unable to attend the world premiere in Oxford, it was quite an experience to see the film in my hometown, at the Loews Theatre downtown. It was a royal homecoming for me and made all the more special by the presence of Clarence Brown. This was one of rare openings where he actually made an appearance. Porter Hall and Elizabeth Patterson were there too, along with half the town, all my friends and family, the press, and even the mayor of Nashville. The applause *Intruder* received meant so much to me because it was a performance—and a story—I took great pride in. A reception at one of the city's most exclusive nightclubs followed the screening.

This night might have been the ultimate highlight of my film career. *The Yearling* premiere was memorable, the Oscar was rewarding, but nothing compared to being the hometown hero.

After *The Yearling*, I had made five films in four years, and the last three had extensive location work. Traveling across the country riding horses could be fun and educational, but it was also exhausting. My mother and sister grew tired of living in Culver City all alone while my father and I stayed away for months at a time, so they packed up and moved back to Nashville.

I didn't blame them for leaving. I was ready to pack up and leave too. On the surface, I appeared to be my smiling, easygoing self, but the creeping dissatisfaction I felt while promoting *The Yearling* was now gnawing away at me on the inside. In September of 1949, I had celebrated my fifteenth birthday on the set of *The Outriders*, surrounded by adult coworkers who were virtual strangers. It struck me that other kids my age probably enjoyed birthday parties with their friends from school. They went to school dances, played sports, and lived much more carefree lives without feeling constant pressure to succeed in the fast-paced Hollywood jungle.

I had endured ups, downs, and mixed feelings about the industry since landing in Hollywood four years earlier. But the set of *The*

Outriders was the first time it occurred to me that the whole setup could be fundamentally unfair. On location with no school and hardly any work, I had plenty of time to think. I pondered what I was doing there in the middle of nowhere. Why was I wedged into this movie as an afterthought? Why was I hardly given a chance to act or make an impression on-screen? The answer was simple enough for a kid to understand: I was under contract to a major film studio whose goal was to make money, like any business. They handed me a paycheck every week. They funded my schooling and drama training. They were determined to get their money's worth. If they didn't have a stellar role for me, they would throw me any old part merely to keep me working and earning my keep. Like countless others who have worked in the movies, my eyes were opening to the unpleasant realities of the glamour factory. I was becoming disillusioned.

Kids react to pressure in different ways. In my case, the anxiety and frustration turned me into a pitiful nail-biter. I compulsively chewed my fingernails down to the quick, until they were bloody and infected. I actually had two nails turn black and fall off. It was gruesome. I don't know if I directly connected my mangled fingernails with working in the movies, but I knew I needed some relief from the nonstop grind. My five-year contract would be up in less than a year, and I was looking forward to joining my mother and sister in Nashville and resuming a less hectic life.

There was one part, however, that I was truly excited about. It was *The Red Badge of Courage,* and acclaimed director John Huston was making it. I loved the novel by Stephen Crane. I could have really sunk my teeth into the role of the Youth, but John Huston insisted on casting Audie Murphy, a young war hero from Texas who was not a trained actor. Huston was so intent on Murphy, he refused to even audition me or anyone else. MGM tried their hardest to get the director to at least consider me, but he was adamant. Though Murphy turned in a convincing performance, test screenings failed to click with audiences. The studio chopped it down to seventy minutes and added narration from the book; Huston felt his masterpiece was destroyed. The movie was a failure.

The Red Badge of Courage was the last role I fought for. When it passed me by, I didn't wait for my contract to officially end. I knew MGM would not renew it anyway, so they agreed to let me out of the remaining six months so I could move back to Tennessee.

I wanted to leave the business, but like most fifteen-year-olds, I was confused and conflicted. I started thinking that maybe all the clichés about the movie industry were true—that they chewed you up and spit you out. The system used kids while they were cute, then when puberty struck, they tossed them back in the sea like an unwanted fish.

But then again, everyone at MGM had treated me well. I had felt welcomed into Louis B. Mayer's kingdom like one of the family, with no hint of cruelty or abuse. I just felt somehow trampled by the system. Clarence had plucked me from obscurity; I had not chased fame, it had come to me. I was literally put on a train and sent to Culver City like a piece of cargo. Naturally, I was willing—what poor, movie-loving kid would not go be a movie star? But no sooner had my life and family been uprooted that I became an easily replaceable commodity within the studio system. Clarence had cast me in two spectacular movies. He had been like a second father to me, so patient as I learned my craft. For that I will always be grateful. But after he moved on to other projects, I could not help but feel pangs of abandonment. He gave me a career, then left me floundering in subsequent mediocre pictures for a factory that did not nurture or guide me as only a caring mentor could.

Was I finished with Hollywood, or was it finished with me? The feeling seemed to be mutual. They simply hadn't known what to do with me since *The Yearling*. Once I became a teenager, I was even less marketable. Until rock and roll exploded in 1955, there was virtually no teen culture in America. No movies aimed at teens and certainly no Disney Channel. Good roles for teenage boys were practically nonexistent. I felt no great sense of loss in leaving Metro-Goldwyn-Mayer behind. In fact, more than anything, I felt relieved.

My father, on the other hand, was shattered.

Until the studio failed to renew my contract in 1949, I don't think I realized how important my Hollywood career was to my father. Like most men of the era, he kept his emotions tightly reigned; I had never seen him cry. When I left MGM, he cried openly.

At the time, I didn't understand why he was devastated. I had made a fair amount of money for the family and had received some acclaim. Our Hollywood years had been an adventure, but it was time to move on. Why was my dad so hurt? It wasn't until years later, shortly before he died, that I discovered what made Claude Jarman Sr.'s life so tragic. He had struggled to overcome the disadvantages of his youth and succeeded in going from dirt-poor country boy in Bell Buckle to a hardworking young man with the prettiest wife in town. They then relocated to the up-and-coming city of Nashville. He must have envisioned his life as an upward trajectory—until the Depression hit, and it hit hard. My father probably had big dreams, but the economic crisis stopped a lot of dreams in their tracks. He took a job as a bank clerk.

I will never know the exact circumstances, but one evening when the bank closed, his drawer came up substantially short of funds. It may have been an honest mistake, or he may have succumbed to a moment of desperation, of feeling trapped by his low salary and fears of supporting a wife with a baby on the way. He carried that secret to his grave. Whatever explanations my father offered, the bank manager either did not believe or did not care. Dad was not only fired, but his reputation was tainted. The incident blackened his record; he was never able to escape it or live it down. His hopes of advancement in the banking field crushed, he was left to take odd jobs he was not particularly qualified to do.

Imagine his elation when, out of the blue, his son was discovered and whisked away to Hollywood with a five-year contract, with Dad on the payroll as chaperone. It must have felt like he'd been granted a reprieve, like God had sent a golden opportunity down from above, a second chance for him to make good. His job with the railroad was not high-paying, but it was steady. Had he stayed, he might have been promoted or eventually collected a pension. But he quit the railroad and did his best to navigate the challenging world of Hollywood for nearly five years.

When it was over, he was forty-five. He was forced to return home and start all over from scratch.

My father's experience in Los Angeles had done nothing to further his career or broaden his job prospects in Nashville. Sadly, he was once again relegated to scraping by in whatever nine-to-five jobs he could obtain. His own destiny went unfulfilled, partly because he had to stop in the middle of his life and supervise me and my film career. My leaving MGM was painful for him, but once we got back to Nashville, I never heard him complain. He took a desk job with the State of Tennessee and quietly settled back into his old routine. It was quite a comedown from the bright lights of Hollywood, USA.

Dad continued to work hard until 1968, when he suffered a massive stroke. He never recovered his speech or other functions and died five months later at only sixty-four. I often wish I could have helped make his life more comfortable while he was alive.

It would have been better for my father if I had been hungrier for fame. Had I been one of the lucky, ambitious handful of young actors who overcomes the awkward years to become a Liz Taylor–level star, my family might have been better off. But I just couldn't do it. That wasn't me. I wanted to live like a regular kid, not be boiled alive by the studio pressure-cooker. It was stressful, and the older I grew, the more artificial it seemed to me. I yearned for reality, not make-believe.

I had saved enough money from my movie work to attend a private boys' school in Nashville. I was just settling into a routine myself—making new friends, focusing on my studies—when MGM called. "Would you be interested in returning for another picture?"

Though I was no longer under contract, they knew and trusted me and thought I was perfect to play a young David Brian in a Western called *Inside Straight*.

Apparently, Hollywood was not finished with me yet.

CHAPTER 7

The Empire Turns to Dust

Inside Straight was more of an adventure-drama set in the Old West than a typical Western. It was the type of film they used to refer to as a "programmer," meaning it adequately filled the demand for product but was not likely to win any awards. Gerald Mayer—the nephew of none other than Louis B. himself—was the director. I was aware of the relation (and the concept of nepotism), but I could not fault Gerald. He was competent and hands-on and seemed eager to make good as a director. He would go on to a lengthy career in television once the movie business started to slump.

I played a character with the ridiculously improbable name of Rip MacCool. David Brian played the adult Rip, and I was the sixteen-year-old version in a flashback sequence. Arlene Dahl, Barry Sullivan, and talented newcomer Mercedes McCambridge played supporting roles, but as in *The Outriders,* I had no chance to get to know my costars. My only scenes were with Lon Chaney Jr., who was supposed to be a Serbian in the film. They glued a false moustache to his face and made him deliver his lines in what the *Los Angeles Times* called a "stagey accent." Chaney was a nice guy when sober but was a notorious alcoholic who once allegedly told a director, "Get everything you can out of me before 1:00 p.m. because after that I can't guarantee anything." I think he visited bars with some drinking buddies for lunch every day and frequently came back a different person. But I never witnessed any of this on the set of *Inside Straight*. We did our scenes, he went to his dressing room, and I to mine.

This time, I was not bothered by anything that happened on the set. I was no longer a contract employee, and making a movie was a whole different experience. There was no pressure. I had my own life to get back to in Nashville, so I enjoyed visiting the old studio for a couple of weeks. They liked my work, and I liked being a free agent. They discussed future roles for me, planning to cast me as a young college student in *Confidentially Connie,* a romantic comedy starring Van Johnson and Janet Leigh. But it didn't happen; I never worked for Metro-Goldwyn-Mayer again.

I couldn't believe how suddenly the studio went downhill once the threat of television took hold in 1950. The old Metro had started to crumble from the inside when Dore Schary replaced Louis B. Mayer in 1948, but it was a silent shifting of the foundation, nothing obvious. The Supreme Court's anti-trust ruling in 1948 didn't help; the studio was forced to sell off its theater chains. From the outside, MGM still appeared to be in its full glory. But it was only a matter of three years before Mayer was out and the whole system began toppling to the ground.

In 1951, Nicholas Schenck, the head of Loews Inc., supposedly sided with Schary in a disagreement with Mayer, and Mayer accused the two men of plotting to oust him from his own studio. He didn't wait for them to accomplish it. L. B. Mayer resigned from MGM after twenty-seven years as head of production. There was more to it than a mere quarrel. TV was posing a real threat to film. As it had during the talking picture revolution of the late 1920s, the industry panicked. Unlike the talkie crisis, the Hollywood studio system would not survive the TV panic. In 1947, there were only one or two television stations broadcasting, and only about forty-five thousand American families owned a set. By the end of 1949, 4.2 million homes had TV sets. Why should people go out to the movies when they had entertainment right in their living rooms?

When movie profits plummeted, the East Coast banks and businesses that backed the studios cracked down. New York businessmen who knew and cared nothing about filmmaking were flown in to oversee production. The moment the businessmen called the shots, Hollywood became a different kind of town. All across the industry, moguls who had built studios from scratch—the Warner brothers, the Harry Cohns—were losing power and scrambling to stay afloat.

Mayer was the first of the big moguls to be edged out of his own studio. After he left Metro, Mayer continued to count Clarence Brown as one of his closest allies. They still dabbled in film production, sharing a little office on Canon Drive in Beverly Hills. They owned property in the San Fernando Valley and were among the first to build in the city of Palm Springs. Mayer did well in real estate and horse racing, so he was not exactly a pauper. But leaving MGM must have been quite a blow to his ego. He built an empire, ruled over it for a quarter of a century, and then one day, he looked down and saw that it had turned to dust in his hand.

The process may have taken several years, but in my memory, the change was apparent within a matter of months. Even before Mayer left, when I returned to shoot *Inside Straight,* the old MGM was a different place than I had left in 1949. Around every corner, new faces peered at me, most of them cold and unfriendly. Seemingly overnight, the family atmosphere became a hostile, unfamiliar setting. The fun was draining away.

When I first came to the lot in 1945, it was a mini city bustling with creative energy, every stage abuzz with activity. Now, in the wake of cutbacks, it was starting to resemble a ghost town. Soundstages stood dark and empty. Only a few stragglers sat eating in the commissary. My old friend Bob was gone, his shoeshine stand and newsstand closed down. The barber shop was closing its doors too.

Even the old schoolhouse was no more—it had been turned into a producer's office. All the kids under contract at the studio had either grown up or moved on.

Elizabeth Taylor had just turned eighteen and made her debut as a glamorous leading lady in a silly comedy called *The Big Hangover.* MGM missed the mark with that one, but they quickly remedied their mistake by casting Liz as Spencer Tracy's daughter in *Father of the Bride*, a colossal hit that sent her popularity into orbit. Practically overnight, she joined the ranks of the Hollywood elite with *A Place in the Sun*. After breaking up with football player Glenn Davis, Liz married Conrad "Nicky" Hilton in a very press-savvy 1950 ceremony (which, for some reason, I sent a present instead of attending), kicking off a string of highly publicized marriages, divorces, and personal drama.

Jane Powell had also graduated into mature roles at MGM. Jane married before Liz (in 1949), and her career took off when she was paired with Fred Astaire in *Royal Wedding*. In 1954, her stardom would hit an all-time high with the Oscar-winning musical *Seven Brides for Seven Brothers*.

Roddy McDowall and Dean Stockwell both saw their child stardom dissolve as they reached their teens, but each handled it differently. Roddy stayed in the industry, working quietly but prolifically in theater and TV until his adult career was ignited in the 1960s with notable roles in *Cleopatra* and the popular *Planet of the Apes* film series. Dean left show business behind entirely, dropping out of sight for decades until he was in his fifties. Then, in the 1980s, he enjoyed a second career as a character actor in films for acclaimed directors like David Lynch and William Friedkin and even won an Oscar nomination for his role in Jonathan Demme's *Married to the Mob*.

Margaret O'Brien had been the biggest of them all. She was not only the top child star in 1940s Hollywood but had been voted the world's most popular movie star in 1946—no small feat for a girl of nine. She was the darling of the MGM lot, adored by all. By 1950, she was gone. This was a child who was named Margaret after the MGM film that made her a star, *Journey for Margaret*. "I'd been going to the studio since I was four, and I felt lost," Margaret said when it was all over.

Shortly after making *Little Women* and *The Secret Garden* in 1949, Margaret and her mother paid MGM to cancel her contract. Like me, she knew they were not planning a renewal; they had no roles for a girl of thirteen. The children's roles were even drying up now that the studio was no longer putting its energy toward family films like the Andy Hardy series. To keep up with public tastes, Dory Schary focused more on big-screen adventure epics like *King Solomon's Mines* and gritty crime dramas like *The Asphalt Jungle.* MGM still produced its share of sugarcoated musicals, but it left the kid stuff to Disney—which is exactly where Margaret was planning to go next. Walt Disney spent years conceiving a dream project, an *Alice in Wonderland* feature film that would combine live actors with animation. Though Disney seemed determined to cast Margaret O'Brien as Alice, terms could never be reached, and eventually the whole project caved in.

Margaret ended up at Columbia in 1951, but the flimsy comedy *Her First Romance* failed to help her transition to teen roles. What a shame that no one could harness all that talent. Margaret could not only cry on cue, she could control the precise amount of tears! Once, when Henry Koster directed her to cry in a scene for *Music for Millions,* she asked, "Do you want the tears just visible in my eyes or rolling down my cheeks?" She was a born professional and a survivor who stayed sane through all the ups and downs. She worked in theater and television through the '50s and is still active on the classic-film circuit today.

So many child stars were not as fortunate as my MGM classmates. Bobby Driscoll was a boy I knew, though not well. He starred in Disney's *Song of the South* and *Treasure Island* and was the model and voice for the animated Peter in *Peter Pan.* Bobby had made sixteen movies by the time he was thirteen and had earned a Juvenile Academy Award for his starring role in the film noir *The Window.* It was heartbreaking to watch him slowly fall apart when his childhood career went into decline. He started using drugs so young that by the time he was thirty, his body gave out from the strain, and he died, anonymous and broke in New York.

Witnessing cautionary tales all around me—kids being mishandled by managers or parents, turning to drugs and alcohol, or suffering when they outgrew their fame—only confirmed my decision to live in Nashville and focus on getting an education. I could see the danger in putting fame and career first, and I was determined to prioritize real life over Hollywood make-believe.

The Hollywood I had known was disappearing anyway.

Once everyone owned a television, the motion picture business was never the same. Good movies were still made, of course, and still are. But the priorities shifted. Moguls like Mayer were interested in making quality entertainment and also making a profit; the profiteers who inherited the business were only interested in the bottom line. Studios could no longer afford to gamble on artistic projects or to keep a village of talent on the payroll. Fewer films were made, fewer people steadily employed.

Actors were no longer pampered, nurtured within a familial environment—but then again, they were not bought, sold, and traded like goods. Maybe the breaking down of the studio system was a painful but healthy progression.

My work on *Inside Straight* wrapped in a few weeks, and I returned to school. I was just settling into Nashville life again when another long-distance phone call came from Hollywood. This time it was not MGM but a representative from producer Merian C. Cooper's office requesting to interview me for a picture to be directed by John Ford. For the first time since my ill-fated attempt to land *The Red Badge of Courage,* I was excited about a movie role. I was well aware of both of these men and impressed with their work.

Though his heyday was before my time, I knew that Merian C. Cooper was a living legend—he was the man behind *King Kong.* Cooper not only directed the film but conceived the idea of a giant ape on a prehistoric island, his imagination sparked by his real adventures as an explorer and a bomber pilot in World War I. The success of *Kong* led Cooper to a prolific career as producer at RKO in the '30s and '40s, then to a stint working with John Ford at Republic Pictures. Republic was the greatest of the low-budget "Poverty Row" studios, a haven for men like Cooper and Ford who liked to work independently of the major studios, with more autonomy and creative freedom. Ford had already made two cavalry-themed pictures there—*Fort Apache* in 1948 and *She Wore a Yellow Ribbon* in 1949— and was planning a third to round out the trilogy.

John Ford had etched a legendary reputation for himself too. He had already taken home three Best Director Oscars by 1950, but more than that, he changed the landscape of American film by resurrecting the Western genre and giving it a new artistic sensibility. Personally, Ford was known as a man's man, a tough hombre who liked to make Westerns using the same stable of actors he trusted. John Wayne headed that list, with supporting players like Ward Bond and Victor McLaglen as part of the posse. I knew *Fort Apache* had featured Shirley Temple as Wayne's daughter, and I heard that her husband John Agar (in his first film role) was relentlessly bullied by Ford. He was an intimidating figure.

I was reluctant to miss a few days of school, especially with final exams on the horizon, but I was not about to turn down Mr. Cooper and Mr. Ford's invitation. My dad and I flew to Los Angeles for the interview. It was my first visit to the Republic lot in Studio City up in the San Fernando Valley.

When I stepped into Merian Cooper's office, there sat the famed Mr. Ford. Dressed in khaki slacks and jacket, he casually smoked a pipe. For what seemed an eternity, he silently eyed me from behind dark sunglasses. If he was trying to unsettle me, I wasn't going to let him succeed. I stood and waited. He finally spoke.

"How are your marks in school?"

"Okay," I replied.

"Can you ride a horse?"

"Yes." I mentioned my work in *Roughshod* and *The Outriders.*

After ten minutes, I was excused and left the office. No acting or emoting, no tests of my dramatic skills. Ford was mainly interested in my athletic abilities.

Next, Jules Goldstone, an agent and attorney who represented me at that time, went into the meeting. After a short time, Jules emerged with the good news. "They want you for the part of John Wayne's son, and you'll be paid $15,000." That was a tidy sum of money in that era and certainly an improvement over my $250 per week at Metro. Furthermore, Ford would be shooting in July and August, so I wouldn't miss any more school. I flew back to Nashville with a smile on my face.

I finished my freshman year at Montgomery Bell Academy and returned to California to prepare for my role in a film that, at that point, was either going to be called *Rio Grande Command* or *Rio Bravo*. Nine years later, Howard Hawks would use *Rio Bravo* as a title for one of his Westerns. Our movie, it was eventually decided, would be called *Rio Grande*.

"John Ford is known for constantly changing the script," I was told by those who knew him, "so be prepared for anything." Sure enough, about three weeks before start of production, Ford called me into his office and said I should learn how to Roman ride—standing astride two horses at once. There was no mention of this in the script, but I knew better than to ask questions. So I headed up to the Fat Jones Stables on a ranch in the valley and spent days learning how to navigate around a track standing up on the backs of two horses. It was a little scary at first but, for a fifteen-year-old, quite a thrill.

My first day at the ranch, I met two actors who would become my best friends on the set, Ben Johnson and Harry Carey Jr. All three of us had to learn to "ride like them ancient Romans," to quote a line from the movie. Ben was an exceptional horseman, having started his career as a stuntman and rodeo champion. Harry, who went by the name of Dobe, was, like Ben, part of the Ford family. Dobe was the son of character actor Harry Carey and had grown up on the sets of his dad's Westerns. He even referred to John Ford as "Uncle Jack." Ben and Dobe were about twice my age. They knew I was only fifteen, and they were worried I might hurt myself trying to Roman ride. They seemed as surprised as I was when I stood up without a hitch on my first try! Ben even seemed a little chagrined that I took to trick-riding so easily and was heard to mutter, "The reason that kid did it so easy is that his feet are so goddamned big they just wrapped around the horse's back!"

In mid-July, we all boarded a Douglas DC-6 to Grand Junction, Colorado, and from there took a bus to Moab, Utah. Ford's favorite location was Monument Valley in Arizona, so this was a slight departure. Today, Moab is a hiking and camping destination, but in 1950, it was a lonely dot on the map, a tiny desert oasis just east of the Colorado River. The mercury hovers around 100 degrees in July, but at least it's a dry heat—nothing like the Florida Everglades in the summer. We stayed in a little motel and ate our meals in a tent that was erected for the cast and crew.

There was a certain lifestyle associated with location Westerns, and it fit right into John Ford's life and work ethic. He once described why he loved making Westerns: "You get up early in the morning and go out on location and work hard all day and then you come home and you go to bed early. It's a great life." And Mr. Ford had the lifestyle down pat. A veteran of over a hundred films at that time, he knew exactly what he wanted and got it quickly and efficiently, with minimal waste and no sense of urgency or panic. Dobe Carey called *Rio Grande* a "vacation picture" for Ford, meaning it was summertime and his pace was more relaxed than usual.

With Ben Johnson and Harry Carey Jr., *"Rio Grande"*

This did not necessarily make him easier to work for. Ford was notoriously cranky, with an air of mystery about him. I could never tell how seriously to take him. He chewed on a handkerchief constantly, and his eyes were always hidden by those dark glasses. No one could ever determine for sure who he was looking at. It was his custom to select a favorite actor and one that he would harass. This time I was the chosen one, primarily because I was able to conquer Roman riding without any trouble. For some reason, Ben was the scapegoat of the *Rio Grande* set. Ford criticized him constantly for his dialogue flubs, calling him "stupid" in front of everybody. He could be merciless.

Even Duke himself was not exempt from the director's temper. He had been treated cruelly by Ford in the early days of their partnership, before bit-player Marion Morrison became icon John Wayne. But Wayne hung in there and gradually the two proud men formed a powerful bond, resulting in a partnership that spanned forty years and twelve movies. As the top name in the business, Wayne commanded a huge salary but took less money to work with Ford because the quality of his work was unsurpassed. Yet Ford still belittled Wayne when the mood struck. Henry Fonda apparently had the same problem with Ford and eventually stopped working for the director. I noticed that no one in the cast or crew took the director's bullying seriously; they just accepted it as part of the Ford family experience.

One day, I saw what a formidable duo Wayne and Ford could be when they teamed up against someone. The founder and president of Republic Pictures was a hard-boiled character named Herbert Yates, who had gotten on John Wayne's bad side by supposedly welching on a deal he made with the star. Yates had agreed to give Wayne a percentage of the profits from the enormous 1949 hit *Sands of Iwo Jima*, the film that earned Wayne his first Oscar nomination. Apparently, Yates had never paid up. On the set of *Rio Grande*, Wayne went on strike and refused to work until Yates gave him his money. John Ford shut down production for a couple of days. When Yates showed up, Ford growled at him, "When you quit messing with my hired help, I'll go to work again!"

I didn't meet the film's stars, John Wayne and Maureen O'Hara, until the first day of shooting. Wayne was just as he appears up on the screen—bigger than life. I was well over six feet and still growing, but I was a shrimp compared to John Wayne. He towered over us all and carried himself with a certain majestic dignity. He reminded me of Bambi's father in that famous movie. There was no doubt about it, he was the man; all business, thoroughly prepared, and never flubbed his lines. I felt honored to have earned his and Ford's respect.

In the film, Wayne played a US Cavalry colonel, and I was his estranged son, Jeff, a young officer suddenly under his father's command. My mother was played by Maureen O'Hara, the greatest movie mother anyone could ask for. Not only was she a lovely and gifted actress, but warm, genteel, and kind. I was fortunate to have so many scenes with her; she was so natural, she made it easy for an actor to respond naturally. It was my impression that John Ford adored her as much as we all did. It seemed to me that she was Ford's favorite and that, in his eyes, she could do no wrong. Maureen remembered it differently, later revealing that he often quietly insulted under his breath while directing her, saying things like, "Why don't you lift your goddamned head up a little more and get it right? Can't you manage that?" I guess nobody really escaped Ford's needling on that set except me. I will never know why I got so lucky.

Working with Ford's stable of character actors was a treat. I was reunited with my *Yearling* costar, the always colorful Chill Wills, and was introduced to Victor McLaglen, an Englishman full of so many tall tales nobody knew which one to believe. He claimed to be the heavyweight boxing champion of Canada at eighteen, the former police chief of Baghdad, a Boer War hero, and on and on. What a character.

A high point of the film for me was listening to the Sons of the Pioneers sing their songs. They were a vocal group originally formed by cowboy star Roy Rogers, and they performed in *Rio Grande* as the Regimental Singers. Ken Curtis, who sang lead at that time, had a gorgeous tenor voice. He had replaced Frank Sinatra as lead vocalist with Tommy Dorsey's band but found greater success in John Ford's Westerns. He even married Ford's daughter Barbara in 1952. He stayed with acting, playing the memorably comic role of Charlie McCorry in *The Searchers,* and went on to small-screen fame as James Arness's sidekick, Festus, in the series *Gunsmoke.*

With John Wayne, *"Rio Grande"* in 1950

Stan Jones composed the music and also had a role in the film. Stan's most famous song was "Ghost Riders in the Sky," the record I played so many times on the jukebox in Oxford that my father grew to hate it. I think Dad finally appreciated Stan's music when he came face-to-face with him on the set. In fact, my father and Stan Jones, the man he said he wanted to strangle, became good friends.

In stark contrast to my last two films where I had been virtually invisible, the *Rio Grande* set was filled with friends, laughter, music, and the best time I've ever had making a movie. I hated to see that summer come to an end. Back in Nashville, I celebrated my sixteenth birthday and returned to school for my sophomore year.

When the film was released in November, the *New York Times* said the "public will eat it up." They certainly did. Ford's epic did not disappoint, and I was even pleased with my role and my own work this time. Of the eleven motion pictures that I appeared in, none has proven to be more recognizable than *Rio Grande*. It remains a classic crowd-pleaser and has secured an important place in history as the third in Ford's Cavalry trilogy. With John Wayne still topping lists of all-time great movie stars and John Ford earning more acclaim with each passing year, it seems *Rio Grande* will have a loyal audience for a long time.

Harry Carey Jr., John Wayne, Maureen O'Hara,
Claude Jarman Jr. and Ben Johnson
-*"Rio Grande"* 1950

December 8, 1950. The day after Pearl Harbor Remembrance Day and just a few weeks after the eagerly anticipated debut of *Rio Grande.* I had recently gotten my license and was driving in downtown Nashville with a classmate of mine. It was dark, foggy, and drizzling rain. We were on Sixteenth Avenue, a street we used to call Record Row, where all the music companies and recording studios are.

The rain was raging like a monsoon. Visibility was so low that, even with my windshield wipers going their fastest, I never saw the taillights of a bus as it pulled over to let someone off.

I saw no one crossing the street in the middle of the block. Suddenly, my car collided with something. I slammed on the brakes and skidded to a stop. I had no idea what I had hit and prayed it was not a person.

When I opened the car door and stepped into the cold, wet night, it was worse than I feared. A small crowd was gathering around the motionless body on the pavement. An ambulance was called, but it was already too late. I read in the paper the next morning that a fifty-seven-year-old local woman, a schoolteacher, had gotten off the bus and tried to cross the street. I still don't understand exactly how it happened. I was not speeding or driving recklessly; I had not run a red light or missed a stop sign. There was simply a sudden impact, and a woman was fatally struck by my car. She died right there at the scene.

I was overcome with grief. It was all so unexpected that I was thrown into a state of shock. The image of that poor woman lying there in the street haunted my mind. I soon found out she was the grandmother of a kid I went to school with. By the time I got back home, the accident had already been broadcast on the TV and radio news. Some of my closest friends heard it and were waiting in our living room to offer their support and compassion. I felt reassured knowing I had friends to rely on.

If the accident had happened to a teen actor today, the news would be everywhere—saturating the Internet universe and cable news channels, spreading across the globe within minutes of the collision. A famous kid would have his career ruined today. He could never live it down.

Back then, there was some national coverage, but it was fairly minimal. A few articles appeared in the newspapers in Los Angeles and other major cities, short pieces with headlines like "Boy Actor Jarman Held in Auto Death." Of course, the local Nashville press reported every detail. But that was it. I was no longer under contract, so MGM had no say in the matter. No Howard Strickling or Eddie Mannix to fly in and fix this. The newspapers merely reported the truth: that Claude Jarman Jr. had accidentally struck and killed a schoolteacher and was found not at fault. End of story.

But it was harder for me to forget and move on. There was an inquiry in which I had to go before the District Attorney and state my side of the incident for the record. When my father and I arrived at the courthouse, a newspaper photographer appeared, snapping pictures without our permission. We hadn't expected that. "I was told the papers were not going to send anyone to take pictures," my father said. "I apologize," said the photographer, "but they did."

The DA assured me that witnesses and police at the scene were convinced that I was not at fault; it was simply a tragic accident. There was nothing I could have done differently. But it's still a difficult concept for a sixteen-year-old boy to process. Because we were both in the wrong place at the wrong time, this innocent woman had her life taken away in an instant, and my adult life was just beginning. I felt both guilty and victimized. I had done nothing wrong, but somehow something awful had happened. It was a surreal detour in my journey.

It took me a while to be able to climb behind the wheel of a car and not mentally relive that night and the accident. It took me even longer to be able to talk about it. After more than seventy-five years, I can write about it, but not easily. The grief stays with me to this day.

The accident haunted my thoughts for a long time. If she had started crossing the street two seconds sooner, or if I had gotten in my car two seconds later, it never would have happened.

She was two-thirds of the way across the street when the edge of my car struck her. I couldn't make sense of it. I went to the funeral and offered my condolences to her grandson. But what more was I supposed to say? What could I do?

The next week at school, my football coach sat me down and talked to me. "The only thing you can do is learn from the experience and move on with your life," he advised. There was nothing else to do. I moved on.

CHAPTER 8

Life Lessons from Lee Marvin

Tennessee was a world away from Hollywood. My life shifted into a more comfortable gear.

Montgomery Bell Academy was a boys' school, and competitive sports played a key role in our education and social lives. I quickly lost interest in acting as athletics took center stage in my world. I played quarterback on the football team, center in basketball, and first base on the baseball team. I was even voted Most Athletic in the school in my senior year. Harpeth Hall, a neighboring girls' school, provided us with dates for our dances and cheerleaders for our games. In later years, Reese Witherspoon attended Harpeth Hall and was one of the cheerleaders.

It was the early 1950s, the era of crew cuts and varsity sweaters, an idyllic time to be young, go on dates, play sports, and lead a fairly normal life. I still worked in movies occasionally, making three more films after *Rio Grande*. But I no longer actively sought roles. In fact, I hated having to miss football games to shoot movies! Like other high school kids, I was motivated by earning extra money during school breaks. The only difference was that I hopped a plane to LA and spent a few weeks in a studio instead of mowing lawns or delivering groceries. In the days before home video and YouTube, movies did not have the longevity they have today; most films came and went from theaters quickly and were soon forgotten. Appearing in some movies did not make me stand out from my classmates. I fit right in.

Toward the end of my senior year, Columbia Pictures offered me a role in another Western. This time I would not play a boy or a kid, but a young man. The film was called *Hangman's Knot,* and I was cast as Jamie, the youngest of a group of Confederate soldiers on the run with a shipment of gold bars at the Civil War's end. It was the most mature part that I'd ever had. Plus, I would only miss three weeks of school, as the entire film would be shot in only eighteen days. Columbia didn't mess around back then.

Hangman's Knot was the brainchild of Roy Huggins, a little-known screenwriter who had aspirations to direct and produce. This tense, character-driven Western was the one and only feature film he would direct in his lengthy, successful career. Huggins went on to create, write, and produce a string of popular TV series including *Maverick, The Fugitive, Baretta,* and *The Rockford Files.* I don't know if he switched to television because he saw the writing on the wall and understood that its future was more lucrative than the waning movie industry. But he was an intelligent, talented man, and I was fortunate to be a part of his directorial debut. He produced commercially appealing entertainment but always tried to inject a little more thought and depth into the material than it might have had in less competent hands.

Randolph Scott was the star of our film and was another highly educated man. By the time we made *Hangman's Knot* in the spring of 1952, he was a seasoned star with over eighty movies to his name, at least half of them Westerns. But he was unique for a Western star—he'd been born into a privileged life as the son of a wealthy Virginia textile manufacturer. After injuring himself playing football for Georgia Tech, Scott went to Hollywood and got work in motion pictures thanks to his father's business associate, none other than Howard Hughes. Randolph Scott was one of the industry's refined gentlemen and holds the distinction of being the only actor admitted into the prestigious Los Angeles Country Club, an organization with a strict policy against accepting show-business people.

Randolph was always utterly professional on the set, impeccably polite and businesslike. He and his wife Patricia had invited me to have dinner in their home before we started the film, and Clarence Brown joined us. Clarence sang my praises, and Randolph shook my hand with a hearty "Looking forward to working with you." It was a nice way to start a film. I met the movie's other star, the beautiful Donna Reed, when I arrived at our location—the Alabama Hills in Lone Pine, California, near Death Valley. Donna reminded me a little of Maureen O'Hara, very kind and ladylike, with perhaps a little more reserve than Maureen. She was one year away from the movie that would win her an Oscar, *From Here to Eternity.*

As much respect I had for Mr. Scott and Ms. Reed, at seventeen they were too sophisticated and all-business for my tastes. I was now old enough to work on location without my father coming along as a chaperone. Dad stayed back in Nashville, but among the cast, I found a new strong male figure in my life: a young unknown actor named Lee Marvin.

Lee was a twenty-seven-year-old ex-Marine whose Hollywood career was on the verge of taking off. In fact, *Hangman's Knot* was his breakout film. It was not only his biggest role to date, but his first bad-guy and his first Western. He would later become associated with Western bad guys after *Bad Day at Black Rock, The Man Who Shot Liberty Valance,* and his comic role in *Cat Ballou,* the movie that won him an Academy Award for Best Actor. Back then, he was just starting out. I was ten years his junior, and I loved hanging around with Lee.

There was a reason John Ford cast Lee alongside John Wayne three times. He could hold his own on-screen with Duke and even reminded me a little of Wayne. He was bigger than life, a powerful presence. Lee was also funny and fun to be around. For one reason or another, he took a liking to me, and we just clicked. During the course of the film, his character gets nastier and nastier, until finally my character shoots him to save Randolph Scott's life. Lee was a good guy, not a villain, yet off-screen he was a little like the bad guys he played so well. He was rough and tumble and unvarnished, a man's man who shot straight from the hip. As a teenage boy, I was impressed by his attitude.

He wanted to take me under his wing and show me the ropes, and I drank in every piece of advice he offered. He had an aggressive philosophy. "You've got to grab what you want in this life," he used to tell me. Like Marlon Brando would say a couple of years later in *On the Waterfront*, "Do it to him before he does it to you." To me, Lee was a dose of earthiness I felt the often-artificial film industry needed. Despite our age difference, we became close friends during and after the movie we made. Whenever I was in Los Angeles, we would get together and go cruising around Hollywood in his Thunderbird. I remember one time we were rolling down Hollywood Boulevard. Lee had been married to his first wife for about a year. With the air of a Zen master imparting a sacred piece of wisdom to his student, he said, "You know, when I got married, thought I'd stop jacking off. But it hasn't happened." Much of what Lee said could be classified as "too much information," but he was authentic, unfiltered—a true original.

Years later, after I moved to San Francisco, Lee called me and let me know he was in town shooting what might have been his most memorable starring role, as a gangster hell-bent on revenge in *Point Blank.* I went to visit him at the St. Francis Hotel, where he was staying with his dad. He was glad to see me, as always, and the same old Lee—except I noticed he was drinking a lot. This was 1966, fourteen years after *Hangman's Knot.* On that early film, I never saw him touch a drop. It was disheartening to see him succumb to heavy drinking and smoking, a lifestyle that would contribute to his death at only sixty-three.

I remember Lee Marvin as he was when I first met him: full of bravado. I guess he was just about my favorite actor I ever worked with because he was the only one who treated me as a peer. He never talked down to me, never dismissed me as "just a kid." His confidence bolstered me, gave me strength going forward in my life into young adulthood. Ultimately, he may not have been the best role model for a teenage boy, considering his alcoholism and the infamous palimony suit against him in the 1970s. But being a kid with one foot in Hollywood and one foot in Tennessee—and having conflicting feelings about the industry and what I wanted to do with my life—he was so cocksure, he made me feel like he had all the answers. Here was a real man who knew what he wanted and how to get it. I credit Lee with inspiring a take-charge attitude in me that propelled me forward in all areas of my life.

Hangman's Knot did fair business, though it received some critical backlash because of its violence. It was something of an early prototype for later Westerns in the 1960s and '70s, grittier and more callous than the typical romantic 1950s Western. I was pleased with the movie but not so pleased with my grades at school. I had to miss the tail-end of my senior year just before final exams and ended up graduating with mediocre test scores and a lower GPA than if I had stayed in school.

In a sense, I was lucky to have a chance to go to Hollywood and work in the movies. How many kids get plucked from the classroom and handed an Oscar-winning role at age ten? But looking at it from the perspective of getting a good education, working in Hollywood did me no favors—except to provide me with the money to afford better schools. Out of twenty-five boys in my graduating class, ten would become doctors. My classmates were dedicated, ambitious young men who had been planning their career paths from a young age. Compared to them, I was horribly unprepared. My school years had been so interrupted that I didn't even apply to college until late in my senior year, nor had I given serious consideration to what my major would be.

All my buddies went to Vanderbilt University in Nashville, so I applied too and was fortunate to be accepted. I knew I did not want to be a professional actor. But what did I want to be? The summer between high school and college, I got an offer to work for Republic Pictures again and irascible old Herbert Yates. Yates was planning one of his quickie B-pictures and wanted John Wayne to star but couldn't get him. Wayne was just finishing up *The Quiet Man* for Ford and heading over to Warner Bros. to make *Island in the Sky* for William Wellman. Somehow, Fred MacMurray wound up with the lead role in an adventure picture called *Fair Wind to Java*.

Fair Wind to Java is, without a doubt, the worst film I ever appeared in. Yates was married to Vera Ralston, a Czech ice skating champion whom he tried repeatedly to make into a big star. The fact that Ralston was neither the most beautiful nor the most talented woman in Hollywood didn't stop Yates from casting her as the love interest of John Wayne, Brian Donlevy, David Brian, and others in a string of not-so-hot pictures. In 1980, the Golden Turkey Awards nominated Vera Ralston for the honor of Worst Actress of All Time. She lost the award to Raquel Welch, but it was a close race.

For this movie, Yates covered his wife's blonde hair with a long black wig and cast her as an Indonesian slave girl named Kim Kim, her Eastern European accent notwithstanding. Ralston's love interest was Fred MacMurray, a once-solid male star of the 1930s and '40s who seemed mystified as to how he got roped into such a turkey. Fred had costarred with Errol Flynn in *Dive Bomber* and played opposite Rosalind Russell, Barbara Stanwyck, and Carole Lombard in some classic screwball comedies. In 1944, Billy Wilder gave him his most iconic role, salesman Walter Neff in *Double Indemnity.* Fred was well-liked in the industry, but when the studio system fell apart, he got less and less work. He was another casualty of a system that transformed obscure folks into celluloid heroes, then dumped them when their best years had been spent. Like many other golden-era movie stars, he ultimately turned to television, finding fame as Steve Douglas on the long-running sitcom *My Three Sons.*

Fred was just as he appears on-screen. He was a down-to-earth, easygoing guy. I remember being on set with Fred while Vera Ralston was shooting an exotic dance number. He looked at me, glanced at Ralston, and shook his head in disbelief. "I must be crazy for making this movie," he said under his breath, as much to himself as to me.

I knew how he felt. I have no idea what I was doing in that movie. Fred played a ship's captain who discovers a savage slave girl shackled below decks. Naturally, he falls madly in love with her as they go pearl-hunting in Java. I played a guy named Chess who has no bearing whatsoever on the plot. For me, it was just a chance to earn some cash. Though it was a B-picture, Herbert Yates was known to overspend on vehicles for his wife. I was paid $7,500 to be a deckhand. I doubt if the movie even grossed enough to justify the expense. The whole thing was a joke. It took place on an exotic island but was shot on the Republic back lot, fake volcano and all. The *New York Times* seemed to enjoy lavishing adjectives like "gaudy," "clichéd," and "inane" on the film.

In one sequence, Ms. Ralston was stripped naked and whipped in a torture dungeon. Of course, she wasn't fully exposed to the camera—but it makes you wonder what kind of a man enlists his wife to play such a scene. I don't think it's been shown in decades, but if *Fair Wind to Java* ever surfaces, it will be as a campy cult classic.

I took my paycheck and headed straight back to Nashville. I started college, studying liberal arts, history, and political science at Vanderbilt. My poli-sci professor was Lee McClain, a speech writer for local Democratic politician Estes Kefauver. He was aware that I had experienced a certain degree of Hollywood fame, and he urged me to make a public speech supporting the senator. "Will you make a speech for Senator Kefauver?" he kept asking me. The way he phrased it, I assumed it was a legitimate question. Not quite. It was, in fact, a demand disguised as a question. I politely said no and promptly received a failing grade in the class. I went back to Prof. McClain and agreed to make the speech. My grade shot up to an A.

I was learning a lot about politics and how the world worked. I was getting an inkling of ways I could use my background in film to my advantage without having to be an actor or a director. I was drifting further away from any ambitions to work directly in the filmmaking industry, yet I still had an interest in motion pictures.

It had been three years since I stepped in front of a camera when I got another call for a movie during my senior year in college. Walt Disney Studios wanted to cast me as Jacob Parrott in *The Great Locomotive Chase,* a live-action feature based on a real historical event from the Civil War, when a group of Union soldiers disguised as Confederates hijacked a train and took it across enemy lines. Parrott was captured and tortured in the original raid in 1862 and was the first ever recipient of the Medal of Honor. It sounded like a good story, plus it was an opportunity to hang out with my old *Rio Grande* buddy Dobe Carey, who costarred in the film. I accepted. It would be the last movie I ever made.

Clayton, Georgia—where they later shot *Deliverance*—was our location. It was truly *Deliverance* country, a real backwoods town on the banks of the Chattanooga River crawling with colorful Southern characters. Dobe and I joined in the local custom by driving across the county line every night to drink beer or moonshine. This is what the Clayton folks did—their county was dry, meaning no alcohol could be sold or purchased.

Fess Parker was the star of the film. Most people today have forgotten how famous he was, but he was a major Disney discovery. When they cast him as Davy in the 1955 TV series *Davy Crockett,* he became instantly idolized by kids everywhere. Suddenly every little boy in America wore a coonskin cap and sang the words to "The Ballad of Davy Crockett," the theme song that was a number-one hit. But Parker was under exclusive contract to Disney, and they quickly typecast him by starring him in a string of forgettable Western and adventure pictures aimed at youngsters. Until they struck gold with *Pollyanna* in 1960 and hit the jackpot with *Mary Poppins* in 1964, Disney was not entirely successful at attempting live-action films. That didn't stop them from trying.

My role was a minor one. I didn't mingle much with the principal players, Fess Parker, Jeffrey Hunter, and the star of Howard Hawks's sci-fi classic *The Thing from Another World,* Kenneth Tobey. Another *Rio Grande* cohort, Stan Jones, did the music for the film.

Clayton County has become something of a film-location hub in recent years—a *Hunger Games* sequel was shot there—but it was nothing of the kind back when our crew descended upon it in late 1955. We were all jammed into the same small hotel, the only one in town. My roommate was a young actor named Dick Sargent. Dick was just starting out in small bit parts and wouldn't get his big break until 1969, when he replaced Dick York as Darrin Stephens on the TV series *Bewitched.* He was just getting a foothold on his career as I was wrapping mine up. He was a great guy. When we returned to California for the final month of filming, I rented an apartment in Westwood, and he gave me a ride to the set every day. Like Van

Johnson, he was gay but closeted at the time. No one suspected. I kept up with him over the years and was saddened when he succumbed to cancer at only sixty-three—the same age as Lee Marvin when he died. They were both way too young.

Walt Disney was going through his train obsession at the time he produced *The Great Locomotive Chase*. He had constructed miniature railroads at home in his backyard and had just put the finishing touches on a much more elaborate railroad for Disneyland, the Southern California landmark he had opened earlier that year. For *Locomotive Chase*, Disney had high ambitions and an exciting, fact-based story. I figured Walt was personally attached to the project when I saw him arrive on the set to check out the production. He traveled all the way to Georgia to give the film his personal approval. He seemed interested in every detail and enthusiastic about the outcome. It actually did fairly well at the box office, and I'm surprised it isn't better known today.

In 1959, John Ford stock company actor Ward Bond got me a role on his TV series *Wagon Train*. I had never done television before. What a come-down from the movies! In those days, TV production was nothing like filmmaking. Episodes were shot on shoestring budgets at a lightning-fast pace. I was shocked at how little time we had to prepare; minutes after being handed the script, it seemed actors were expected to be fully in character and ready to shoot. I made it through the episode but felt out of my depth and lost. This time, I was really finished with acting.

For me, the transition from studio life to normal life was a good thing. I sometimes wonder what it would be like if I stayed in Hollywood. With enough work and enough luck, I might have gotten a role TV series that lasted a few seasons. But I had no interest in being a TV star.

Besides, Hollywood was not the same. For those of us who had tasted the bygone studio days, like Janet Leigh once said, "Nothing will ever be like that again."

CHAPTER 9

An Hour Away from Hollywood

By the time I turned twenty, the glory of the Hollywood studio system was nothing but a distant memory. A brand-new cultural phenomenon was blossoming to take its place. The focus was shifting from old to young, from Los Angeles to San Francisco. The Bay Area was the birthplace of the sixties counterculture movement, and I witnessed it all.

But it came as a surprise. I had no such plans when I finished *The Great Locomotive Chase* and returned to Vanderbilt in December of 1955. In fact, my plans to graduate college almost didn't pan out. Because I had missed practically all of the first quarter, I was not permitted to take my exams and was forced to increase my course load in order to graduate in June of 1956. I just made it by the skin of my teeth.

I was now free to start a life for myself but unsure which path to take. Part of me wanted to stay away from Hollywood—yet all my professional experience had been in the movie industry. This was what I knew. I had been trained and nurtured by the likes of Clarence Brown and John Ford, the best in the business. I was often bitten by a fleeting temptation to head back to LA and revive my career. I might have attempted it had the industry been the same as when I started out, when directors like Clarence could spend a whole year crafting a timeless work of art on reels of celluloid film. But that had all evaporated. I eyed the new Hollywood—with its cheaply-made Styrofoam space monsters and its mediocre TV family sitcoms—with much trepidation. Great films were still being made, but they seemed all too few and far between.

The Korean War was still raging, so my dilemma was solved for me by the US government. I would either have to serve two years in the Army and go to Korea or enroll in the Navy Officer Candidate School, become an officer, and serve for three years. I decided to go the Navy route, but my colorblindness was an obstacle; I flunked the necessary physical. I got around this by obtaining a waiver that forbade me from ever commanding a ship. After four months of training in Newport, Rhode Island, I was commissioned to spend two years in Seattle and the last year in Los Angeles.

While in Seattle, I married my Vanderbilt sweetheart, Virginia Murray. By the time we arrived in California, she was expecting our first child. While in LA, I tested the waters by doing guest spots on a few TV series, but my heart still wasn't in it. When my time in the Navy was up, I sought full-time employment in a steady line of work. I had to. Virginia gave birth to a son, Claude III, and I now had a family to support. I fought my father over the name.

"I had to grow up as Little Claude, and I'm not going to saddle my son with the same problem," I told him.

"Well, I hope you will still name him Jarman" was his wounded response.

We settled on a compromise: name him Claude but call him Cal.

In 1959, I took a job with an advertising agency in my wife's hometown of Birmingham, Alabama. At that time, Birmingham was seething with racial strife. Martin Luther King was leading the charge against Bull Connor, the Commissioner of Public Safety. Connor took an aggressive anti-integration stance, enforcing segregation with the use of vicious police dogs and firehoses. His intolerance only served to incite more rage and to perpetuate the cycle of violence. The local press in those days covered up or whitewashed the incidents when Connor set his dogs on protestors. Birmingham newspapers never gave the full story. We had to watch the network news shows to see the truth. Once, after citizens fought back against one of his attack dogs, Bull Connor's response was "I don't know why anyone doesn't like dogs." Birmingham was a city ripping apart at the seams.

After my second son, Murray, was born, an event occurred that changed the course of my life. In my job, I had done some public relations work for John Hancock Life Insurance Company, headquartered in Boston. Looking to expand in the West, they were opening a new office in San Francisco. Heading up the operation was the Western Vice President, Bill Bird. Bill needed an assistant to handle PR and press, and I was offered the position. Neither my wife nor I had ever set foot in San Francisco. With two toddlers under age two, we accepted the challenge and headed west. It was not just a new adventure and a chance to carve out a fresh career path and earn more money—it was way out of the daily chaos of living in Birmingham. It had become such a volatile area, we felt unsafe driving in another state with Alabama license plates on our car. Simply being from the South could incite violence in other parts of the country.

Relocating from Civil-Rights-era Alabama to San Francisco was like landing on another planet. Everyone was welcome, and virtually anything was allowed. This was 1961. Bohemia was alive and crazy. It was a little too early for the psychedelic flower-power movement; that would blossom a few years later. When Virginia and I arrived, the scene was still jazz, beat poetry, and coffee shops. For the latest (and the wildest) art and music, it was the place to be. As a hard-working father of two, I had little direct involvement in the creative counterculture. But it surrounded and fascinated me.

As the 1960s and '70s raged on, I had plenty of opportunities to participate in the psychedelic experimentation that abounded in the city, but I was never interested. Maybe it was my conservative Tennessee upbringing or simply an aversion to drugs. One time, a friend offered me a free LSD trip. "I'll drive you around and you can look out the window at all the colors," he volunteered. "No thanks," I said. "I'm colorblind anyway." I passed. Chaos surrounded me during those turbulent years, but I kept it at arm's length.

My job was all-consuming. It involved considerable travel, not only throughout the west but also Boston and New York. After two years, Virginia moved back to Birmingham. I don't think raising two boys practically by herself, on the other side of the continent from her family and friends, was her idea of happily ever after. Our marriage deteriorated into an uneasy state of on-again, off-again separation as all my energy went into my career. It was painful to have a failing marriage and two kids in another state. I coped with the loss by throwing myself even further into my job. I wanted to make good as an adult, to prove I was more than just "Claude Jarman Jr., the kid from *The Yearling* and *Rio Grande*."

In 1965, a special opportunity came my way. In the 1950s and early '60s, film festivals were rare. In fact, there was only one important festival: the Festival de Cannes in France. There were no significant film festivals in North America until the New York Film Festival got underway in 1963. In 1956, San Francisco theater owner Irving "Bud" Levin teamed with the Italian counsel to host an Italian film festival in celebration of the city's Italian Heritage Week. Federico Fellini's latest film *La Strada* was screened along with other cinematic offerings from Italy. It was such an overwhelming success that it gave birth to the San Francisco International Film Festival, the first major celebration of film in the United States.

The event rapidly outgrew itself. It became so popular it took on momentum of its own but had no one to properly manage it. The press harshly criticized the festival for making some serious gaffes that were embarrassing to the visiting foreign delegations, and thus to the community. What proved to be the final straw occurred on opening night in 1964. The opening reel for the feature film had been misplaced by the festival. The film's director had to stand up and describe the first reel to the audience, to be followed by the second reel, which was loaded and ready to roll. Halfway through the second reel, the first reel was found. Instead of continuing with the film, the second reel was interrupted and the film was started again from the beginning. The reviews were devastating.

Soon after the close of that year's festival, I was on a cross-country flight to Boston with my boss, Bill Bird.

"Something should be done about the San Francisco International Film Festival," I told him. "San Francisco is a cultural metropolis with a great opera, symphony, and ballet. The film festival should become a bright star alongside these icons."

Bird was a creative thinker as well as a spell-binding public speaker. He had recently been elected president of the San Francisco Chamber of Commerce, and he was in the position to offer me a challenge. "Why don't you explore the idea of organizing a committee of people connected to the arts? Your committee can submit a proposal outlining how the Chamber could assume control of the event and guarantee its financial success."

It was not my choice to relocate to San Francisco—my company sent me there. It was not my idea to become involved in a film festival. But it almost felt like fate was pulling the strings in some way, roping me back into the world of Hollywood movies. This time I would work in an entirely different capacity, from the outside looking in. I was much more comfortable there. I accepted Bill Bird's challenge.

I requested a meeting with Bud Levin. The timing, as it turned out, was perfect. The bad press and the difficulties of running the festival had drained him, and he was ready to drop out. He gave me authority to take control while he focused on operating his theaters. I set to work rounding up some of the city's most influential names. Barnaby Conrad was a famed local author who wrote the 1952 novel *Matador* and owned a Bay Area bar named after his celebrated book, The Matador. Conrad had once been Sinclair Lewis's secretary and was widely acknowledged to be a true Renaissance man. Beat-generation author (and close friend of Alan Ginsburg) Herb Gold was recruited, as well as noted writer Niven Busch, who had penned the novel *Duel in the Sun* and the screenplay for *The Postman Always Rings Twice*. Patty Costello, president of the Junior League, was also in.

We still needed someone with real film knowledge and credentials. That led us to Albert Johnson, an Afro-American film historian on the faculty at UC Berkeley. He was a champion of *Intruder in the Dust* and a distinguished scholar of world cinema. Next, seeking a smart businessperson, we recruited Mel Swig of the Fairmont Hotel family. Rounding out our committee was an old Hollywood colleague of mine, the young lady who handed me my pint-sized Oscar back in 1947, Shirley Temple Black. Shirley had retired from acting many years earlier and was then living with her husband in Woodside, California, just south of the city.

Our first order of business was moving the site of the festival to the Masonic Auditorium atop Nob Hill. A more central location than Bud Levin's theater with a seating capacity of 2,200, the Masonic was a logical choice. With the site secured, we convinced the board of the Chamber to underwrite the festival for three years. October was deemed the best month to hold the event; great weather and plenty of tourists. Also, we realized that because the recently-initiated New York Film Festival took place from late September to early October, we could catch their overflow of notable guests.

The 1960s saw an explosion of international cinema: Bergman, Truffaut, and Antonioni were creating masterpieces that overshadowed much of what Hollywood was producing.

European films, particularly from France and Italy, were all the rage. Finally, Albert Johnson, a true genius, could realize his dream of having in-person tributes to distinguished filmmakers and performers from all over the world. As for tributes to classic Hollywood actors and directors, Los Angeles was only an hour away by plane. We were off and running.

We were in awe of how easy it was to get some of the biggest names in the industry to agree to appear at the festival. Remarkably, no one had ever done this before. The Golden Age of Hollywood was the very recent past. Most of its legendary figures were still alive, well, and struggling to remain relevant. Seeing highlights of their best work on the big screen before an appreciative audience was an honor they could not resist. That first year, our list of honorees was mind-blowing: John Ford, Mervyn LeRoy, Busby Berkeley, William Wellman, John Frankenheimer, King Vidor, Leo McCarey, Frank Capra, Bing Crosby, Gene Kelly, and Walt Disney. Albert knew every detail of their histories and could recreate their entire careers—from the early days to current work—by editing together clips of their finest movie scenes.

Contacting this many talented people and securing the rights to screen all their films could sometimes be a challenge. But we had a secret weapon named Shirley. Not only did she have a name famous enough to open any door, but she was an enthusiastic and determined lady. She made several phone calls on behalf of the festival. On one occasion, she tracked down a director all the way to Rio de Janeiro, where he was shooting a film. It was late at night when his hotel room telephone rang. When he picked up the receiver and heard a voice on the other end say, "Hello, this is Shirley Temple," he replied, "You've got to be kidding," and hung up. Shirley, who had a great sense of humor, found this hilarious.

The screenings and tributes went incredibly well, with only one close call. For our homage to Disney, we showed his animated opus *Snow White and the Seven Dwarfs*—but there was a problem shipping the film, and it had not arrived yet. When Barnaby Conrad picked him up at his hotel, the first words Walt Disney spoke as he climbed into the car were "Where's the goddamn film?" Fortunately, it made it there just in time for Walt himself to introduce it. Leo McCarey and Bing Crosby also introduced *Going My Way.* Any festival today—and there are many—would be thrilled to have half the talent we were able to get back then. The only disappointment was the lack of an audience. Our big plans became reality too suddenly to draw big crowds the first couple of years. The cavernous auditorium accentuated the paltriness of the audience. Some tributes drew only about 100 attendees. It was a shame to see the place so empty.

Obviously, there was work to be done. For the next three years, after putting in a full day at John Hancock, instead of going home at five o'clock, I spent a few hours working as a volunteer for the SFIFF every evening. I loved it. I had seen the glory days of Hollywood and had complained when television took over and diminished the film industry. Now I was handed an opportunity to do something about it. In our small way, once a year, we were keeping Hollywood's bygone glory alive by showcasing the best of the classics along with the best of current global cinema. In those early days, we toiled passionately—and for no money—to see the festival take off. Like Mickey Rooney and Judy Garland in an old MGM musical, we were driven by the spirit of "Hey, kids, let's put on a show!"

Everyone seemed on board to make the 1966 festival the greatest event yet. The tributes were once again stellar: Roman Polanski (before his legal troubles), former MGM musical producer Arthur Freed, legendary director George Cukor, and a full afternoon with Fred Astaire.

Unfortunately, one of the key members of our group would leave us that year. When Shirley Temple was informed that we were screening *Night Games,* a Swedish film directed by Mai Zetterling, she refused to have any part of it. Zetterling was a well-known actress and filmmaker influenced by the likes of Ingmar Bergman and Federico Fellini. One controversial scene in the psychological drama depicts a young boy in bed with an adult woman. Today, such an innocent scene would barely merit an R-rating. At the time, many people considered it disgraceful, even pornographic.

Shirley strode into our selection committee meeting and stated, diplomatically but insistently: "I am requesting that this film not be shown at the festival." We told her that we would consider her request, but our committee had no intention of allowing its selections to be censored by Shirley. We voted to keep the film on the program. Shirley essentially handed us an ultimatum: either the film went or she did. As much as we loved and depended upon Shirley, we could not justify allowing her to dictate the selections. She told reporters that the film "merely utilizes pornography for profit." Albert Johnson disagreed. So did the rest of us. Even the *New York Times* found "little in *Night Games* to argue a sound censorship case."

The next thing we knew, Shirley had announced to the press that she was resigning from the board of the festival. All hell broke loose when Shirley Temple fans came out in full force. We received angry phone calls and letters, calling us "old reprobates" and worse. The furor surrounding this film didn't hurt attendance; if anything, it helped publicize the festival. For Shirley, this event launched her political career. The following year, she ran for congress, and in 1969

President Nixon appointed her a UN delegate. She went on to serve as ambassador to Ghana, ambassador to Czechoslovakia, and the first female Chief of Protocol. When she spoke out against the Swedish film, it was clear that she had a legion of devoted supporters who would follow her. She was well-spoken and persuasive. She was made for politics.

When we showed *Night Games,* there was anticipation in the air. The audience was aware of the controversy and on the edge of their seats, waiting to be shocked. In fact, the film was quite tame. There was a sigh of relief mingled with a confused murmuring when the screening was over. Nobody could understand what the uproar was all about.

That year, opening night started with a bang thanks to Jack L. Warner. Everyone knew the Warner Bros. studio head had a reputation for being colorful and outspoken. But what we didn't know when we introduced him before a black-tie audience was that he'd been downing drinks at the bar until he was completely smashed. That evening, we had flown in a special Russian delegation, wining and dining them to ensure more Russian participation in future festivals.

When Jack Warner grabbed the microphone, he unleashed a tirade about "those Commie thugs" in the audience. A staunch anti-Communist, Warner made a fool of himself, ranting against the Red Menace until the crowd started booing and shouting, "Shut up and sit down!" He had to be stopped. Someone was sent to gently pry the microphone from his hand. When Warner felt a hand on his shoulder, he complained, "Someone's goosing me!" Thankfully, the night was saved by the grace of our expert master of ceremonies, Peter Ustinov.

A highlight for me that year was seeing Albert Johnson on stage with Fred Astaire, demonstrating some of the moves that Fred was famous for. Attendance was greatly improved, thanks to Shirley and the press. But the controversy had a sobering effect on the conservative Chamber and the higher-ups at the Masonic temple. When they learned that the event had lost $100,000, they were outraged. They fired the Executive Director they had appointed and asked me to take his place. The only problem? I already had a full-time job. At one point, the mayor of San Francisco, Joe Alioto, intervened, calling the president of John Hancock Insurance to request time off so I could work on the event. "He can't do both" was the president's reply. So I quit my job at the insurance company. I was now Executive Director of the San Francisco International Film Festival.

CHAPTER 10

Surviving the Sixties and Seventies

In 1967, the city of San Francisco exploded with love. I found myself living in ground-zero of the hippie movement. In the summer of '67, Scott McKenzie's hit song "San Francisco" could be heard on everyone's radio: "If you're going to San Francisco / Be sure to wear some flowers in your hair." Hordes of young people took his advice, gathering in the coffee shops of the Haight-Ashbury district, in public parks, and even in the streets. They garnished themselves with flowers and painted their faces in protest of the Vietnam War that was raging on the other side of the globe. There were also plenty of drugs, violent outbursts, and general craziness.

It was the perfect time for our film festival to take off because the prevailing mood was pro-arts and welcoming to other nations. Our goals to make the festival an artistic, multicultural Mecca were taking shape.

Three important figures joined our festival that year. George Gund III was the heir to a wealthy Cleveland banking family who had a fondness for foreign films, particularly Eastern European works. One day, he walked into my office and dropped a $5,000 check on my desk—quite a chunk of money in those days. It proved to me much more than a generous donation; it was the start of a lengthy friendship and a lifelong commitment. George continued to fund the SFIFF until he died in 2016. He was our rock. George saved us so many times when we were in desperate financial straits. He had a genuine passion for films and a benevolent heart.

Some people found George's eccentricities hard to tolerate. He mumbled when he spoke. He was chronically late for meetings. And when George was late, it wasn't just by an hour or two—it was more like a day or two. He practically lived on board his private plane and would plan fishing trips all over the globe for his brother, who was blind. When we traveled to European festivals together each year, George was welcomed like royalty. One time at an event in Communist Moscow during the Cold War, George simply picked up the phone and had salmon flown in from Iceland. The Russians were ecstatic. He was their hero. He was our biggest hero too.

Our second addition was a young woman with political aspirations named Nancy Pelosi. Nancy lent her social connections and planning skills to our gala opening-night reception. Working with Kay Woods, another social powerhouse, she planned the yearly party that served as our major fundraiser (besides George).

Our third newcomer was Charlotte Smith, a sassy blonde from Texas. She took the city by storm with her creativity and enthusiasm. She went on to become Chief of Protocol for the city of San Francisco and the state of California. In later years, she married George Schultz, former Secretary of State under Ronald Reagan.

Our 1967 audience was more boisterous than in the past. Demonstrations in Berkeley and San Francisco generated a shockwave of anti-establishment energy. Suddenly, our seats were filled with college kids who smoked marijuana—and who knows what else—in the back of the darkened theater. Our opening-night emcee was a twenty-nine-year-old who had recently become the youngest news anchor in history, Peter Jennings. The opening film was well-suited to the atmosphere: Richard Lester's *How I Won the War,* a darkly comedic war satire. The star of the movie was John Lennon, who would soon become the musical voice of the anti-war movement.

We paid tribute to a couple of great leading men that year: Henry Fonda and William Holden. Fonda was delighted to be there, the picture of gratitude, with his young wife Shirlee by his side. Holden, by contrast, was not well. He was one of my favorite screen stars, and I was disturbed to see him looking troubled and subdued, so far removed from his confident movie-star persona. He was struggling to conquer the drinking problem that would eventually claim his life. In keeping with our Francophile bent, Jacques Demy and Agnes Varda were both honored.

The turnout had never been better, but the festival was running into other problems. Between the radical new audiences and the shadow of Shirley Temple Black's accusations, the staid Chamber of Commerce had had enough. As soon as their three-year commitment ended, they withdrew all support, and we were left on our own. The Masonic even wanted us out. In stepped our mayor, Joe Alioto. If there ever was a big-city mayor, he was it; charismatic and endlessly making deals. Within a week, Joe had commitments from friends in high places led by theatre magnet Ray Syufy. Good old George Gund took care of the rest. Mayor Alioto then convinced the head of the Masons to give us one more year while the 1,000-seat Palace of Fine Arts auditorium was built. We were back in business.

By the time the Summer of Love began, my first marriage had come to an end. After living apart for a number of years, and several failed attempts to stay together, Virginia and I divorced following the birth of our third child, Elizabeth, in 1966. When I met Maryann de Lichtenberg, a model and former ballerina, I was not thinking of the film festival. But she turned out to be an enormous help in dealing with European delegations. Maryann had been born in Budapest, raised in Switzerland and England, and spoke several foreign languages. We were married in 1968.

That same year, my father died. I went to Nashville and accompanied my mother on her first airplane journey as we flew back to California together. She never drank—not while my father was alive, anyway. On the plane, I ordered a martini and watched in wonder as my mother grabbed the glass from my hand and took a gulp. She was a very reserved woman, but I enjoyed observing her subtle reactions to the freewheeling citizens of San Francisco. She neither smiled nor frowned when she saw the flower children and the Hari Krishnas. She drank in the scene with characteristic stoicism.

By 1968, the festival was being hailed as a truly valuable and unique cultural event. We combined the latest in avant-garde cinema with groundbreaking works from other countries and a healthy dose of appreciation for Hollywood's past triumphs. We kicked the program off with a new Rod Steiger film hosted by Gene Kelly, followed up with offerings by Andy Warhol, Michelangelo Antonioni, and Jean-Luc Goddard, and premiered the Beatles' animated adventure *Yellow Submarine* to American audiences with a midnight showing. Lillian Gish, Edward G. Robinson, Kirk Douglas, William Wyler, and John Huston were on hand for tributes, and Barbra Streisand flew in to accept our first-ever Samuel Goldwyn Award. All 2,200 seats were sold out a week in advance. "The event is well on its way to coming of age," *Los Angeles Times* critic Kevin Thomas wrote. "It has flair, diversity, and best of all, sound organization."

1967 San Francisco Festival with Henry Fonda

The 1969 festival was sheer insanity. The opening-night feature was *The Secret of Santa Vittoria* starring Anthony Quinn and Virna Lisi, a natural for Joe Alioto and his Italian friends. Joe and Anthony

Quinn were across the street having dinner, and I was at the theater greeting the guests who were arriving in their finest evening attire. A catering truck pulled up, and out stepped what appeared to be several waiters carrying trays of meringue pies. I later found out they were a theater troupe looking to have some fun at our expense. Quite a few tuxedos were ruined that night when the "waiters" started hurling pies at our guests! Somehow, I managed to avoid getting creamed. I scurried to a telephone and called Joe: "Don't come over until the coast is clear," I warned. The police came to break up the mess, and the Chief of Police took a pie right in the face. This episode turned out to be more entertaining than the movie that night. Our host for the evening, Victor Borge, opened with the perfect line: "I am so glad to see that we are getting violence off the screen and into the street where it belongs."

I always kept two opening-night tickets in my pocket for unexpected emergencies. That night, I figured it was safe to give them away because the curtain was going up. Just as I handed them to two audience members, Mayor Alioto appeared. "I gave my seat to my daughter," he said, "I need a ticket." What could I do? I gave up my own seat and squeezed into an empty seat among the crowd.

John Schlesinger, Sidney Lumet, Mike Nichols, and Milos Forman were among the guests that year, and Elia Kazan sat in the audience as we screened his wife's movie, *Wanda*. Barbara Loden was one of the few women at that time to write, produce, and direct a feature film. But the overwhelming audience favorite was a legendary lady we never thought we would get, Bette Davis. We had sent invites to her home but had received no response. Out of the blue, we checked our answering machine after lunch one day and heard that unmistakably distinctive voice. "Hello. This is Bette Davis. I would like to come." She was witty, warm, and direct, and she packed the theater to the rafters.

The chaos reached a fever pitch on Halloween night, when we screened *Feast of Friends,* a documentary about the Doors. Jim Morrison was not happy with the film, and neither were his fans. They were loud and raucous, threw things and shouted at the screen, and tipped over trash cans on their way out. The assault on anything the hippies saw as "establishment" was full-blown and could get violent.

1968 Film Festival with Kirk Douglas

Z, a political film by leftist filmmaker Costa-Gavras starring Yves Montand, was a big hit in '69. It would win Academy Award nominations for Best Picture and Best Foreign Film. On the Monday following the close of the festival, Don Rugoff of Cinema V, the US distributor of *Z*, called to ask why his film had not been returned. Our answer was unfortunate but true. "It was stolen right out of the projection booth." It never reappeared.

Somehow, the festival managed to survive the sixties.

The Palace of Fine Arts Theatre was ready in time for the 1970 event. Incredibly, the work had been done in less than a year. Bill Cosby was our emcee, and guests included Martin Ritt, Paul Newman, David Lean, and Rosalind Russell. We were rolling along. Our goal to perpetuate the art of filmmaking by shining a light on its most exciting creations was coming to fruition.

October 1971 was British Trade Week in San Francisco. The Queen's niece Princess Alexandra (snidely referred to in the local press as a "second-string princess") and her husband Angus Ogilvy were in town, so we planned a British theme for the festival. Rex Harrison was honored with a tribute, and Merle Oberon was to appear in person. Once we started viewing her body of work, we realized that, aside from *Wuthering Heights,* her film career was rather slim. Merle had just produced and starred in a feature called *Interval.* "Someone should come down to Los Angeles and screen it," she said. "I think it would make a great opening-night picture." She described the romantic drama in which she played a worldly woman who falls in love with a handsome young artist. It sounded like a vanity project to me. In fact, the sixty-year-old Merle had recently left her husband for her thirty-five-year-old costar, Robert Wolders.

Maryann and I flew down, had dinner with Merle and Robbie, and watched a rough cut of the film. It was worse than I feared. Dreadful was not the right word—more like laughable. The plot was barely discernible beneath layers of silly romantic clichés, including the hero running across a field into his lover's waiting arms. There were quite a few flattering shots of Ms. Oberon, but not much else. She was a lovely and talented woman, but *Interval* was beneath her. What was I going to say?

"I'll discuss the screening with the board," I told her as we left. I broke the news to Joe Alioto as soon as I could. "I think it would be a terrible mistake to screen it. The press would tear it apart, Merle would be embarrassed, and the festival would get the blame for showing it." The mayor agreed. We solved the problem by showing *Wuthering Heights* in its entirety and a brief-as-possible clip from the ill-advised film. Merle and Robbie got married in 1975 and were still married when she died in 1979. Robbie eventually found happiness with Audrey Hepburn and stayed with her until her death in 1993.

Loosely adhering to our UK theme was a midnight showing of short films by John Lennon and Yoko Ono in promotion of Lennon's *Imagine* album. Our non-British offerings for the '71 event included Clint Eastwood introducing his directorial debut *Play Misty for Me,* Vittorio de Sica's *The Garden of Finzi-Continis,* tributes to directors

Arthur Penn and Vincente Minnelli, and *Directed by John Ford,* a documentary by Peter Bogdanovich. I had called Ford, hoping I could persuade him to fly up for the screening. He was his usual contrary self.

"But it's a film all about you and your work," I told him.

"Not interested."

"Well, is there anything I can tell the audience on your behalf? What would you like to me to say about the film?"

"Tell them it wasn't directed by John Ford," he grumbled. Needless to say, the movie was shown without the participation of Mr. Ford. At least he had been present for his 1965 tribute.

Orson Welles, however, was an impossible dream. I had tried for several years to get Welles to the festival, but he completely ignored all forms of correspondence. In 1972, I read in *Variety* that he was in Los Angeles and was staying at the Beverly Hills Hotel. I prepared another invite, boarded a plane, and arrived in person at the hotel. I enlisted the help of the front-desk attendant. "I would like to make sure this envelope is personally delivered to Mr. Welles's suite." It was an official invitation to the festival and a handwritten note from me imploring Mr. Welles to let me buy him lunch. I felt sure that would generate a response. It did indeed. When I flew back to San Francisco and checked the machine, I heard his sonorous voice. "This is Orson Welles. I cannot come to lunch today or ever." Click. I got the message.

We soldiered on without the iconic Welles. But we did manage to get his ex-wife. Our featured actress for 1972 was the red-headed love goddess herself, Rita Hayworth. Of all the illustrious guests we paid tribute to during my years at the festival, none touched my heart quite like this lady. She was my absolute favorite. At fifty-three years old, she was beautiful, but the sadness and strain of her life showed on her face, especially in her eyes. I later learned that she was suffering the early stages of Alzheimer's disease and had been self-medicating by drinking heavily. But when I met her, she was vibrant and funny, earthy and bawdy.

The night she arrived in San Francisco, I took Rita to dinner with her hairdresser. At one point, the conversation turned to travel and railroads. Rita said, "Don't tell me about railroads. I know all about railroads. I've been railroaded all my life." She meant it to be funny, but there was obviously some painful truth in it. This poor woman had been mistreated and taken advantage of by her father, by Harry Cohn at Columbia, and countless others. That night before her tribute, I stood backstage and watched her as the emcee introduced her. All traces of bitterness vanished as she straightened herself up, put her shoulders back, and made a grand entrance. Like Marilyn Monroe, she could switch on the "Rita Hayworth" character at will. And when she turned it on, her charisma was overpowering. Her fans adored her. As Clarence Brown said about Joan Crawford, "What a dame."

San Francisco–based Francis Ford Coppola was the director of the moment. After making *The Godfather,* Coppola took a break from producing *American Graffiti* to make it to our festival that year. We also paid tribute to old masters Raoul Walsh and the legendary Howard Hawks.

We never brought Clarence Brown up for a tribute because it would have been too embarrassing to see myself up there on the screen. It would have felt too self-glorifying. We tried a couple of times to salute Gregory Peck, but he had married a French woman and was spending most of his time in Europe by then. Though I was never interested in watching or reviving the films I had appeared in as a child actor, I was still a child of old Hollywood. I was gratified to see the outpouring of affection for the stars and films of the past.

The tributes were wildly popular and had always been free to the public. I felt strongly that we should start charging a small admission fee. The festival needed the money, and by issuing tickets, we could close the theatre when we reached capacity. Albert Johnson, true to his Berkeley roots, insisted they remain free. I had great respect for Albert, but I had to argue that keeping the tributes free was impractical. At the press conference after the 1972 festival, Albert threw me a curve. He announced that he would resign if the festival insisted on charging for tributes. That was not negotiable. As we had when Shirley issued her ultimatum years ago, we let him walk. The press reaction was divided, but we stood our ground. We approached

Pauline Kael in our search for a replacement, but she demurred. We finally settled on a young New York film historian named Marty Rubin. Marty was a terrific talent and a team player.

After eight years, you'd think we would be used to attracting top-tier talent, but we were continually surprised at the quality of guests we were able to procure. Our 1973 lineup consisted of Joanne Woodward, Ruth Gordon, Robert Altman, Shirley MacLaine, and one of our favorites, French director Francois Truffaut. He brought his latest film *Day for Night* and its star, Jacqueline Bisset. When she accompanied Truffaut on stage for his tribute, the emcee gave her name a French twist: "Jacqueline Beee-zay." She grabbed the microphone and declared, "I am English, and my name is Biss-it!" The emcee stood corrected.

Documentarian David L. Wolper was another honoree, along with two young women directors from France, Anna Karina (with her film *Vivre Ensemble),* and Mireille Dansereau (with her film *Dream Life).* Actress Jeanne Moreau made the first of many visits to the festival that year. She loved participating in the screenings and discussions and embodied everything we wanted the event to be. She became a fixture.

The Vietnam War was drawing to a close in 1974 but was still being fought and protested. As the number of casualties climbed, Americans grew disgusted with seeing violent deaths on their TV news every night. San Franciscans in particular became fiercely opposed to violence. We opened the 1974 festival with the anti-Nazi thriller *The Odessa File,* starring Max Schell and Jon Voight, and also premiered the brilliant Vietnam War documentary *Hearts and Minds,* both in keeping with the mood.

As a last-minute surprise, Martin Scorsese showed up with his breakout film *Mean Streets.* Scorsese was one of a new crop of filmmakers who had stripped away the glamour of studio-era Hollywood and replaced it with a raw and gritty realism born of the New York streets. This created a problem for our festival. The anti-violence backlash was so strong that no one wanted to interview Scorsese, and our audience was not very receptive to his style. We were finally able to get one of our assistant program managers to take on the job, but it was embarrassing. The cool lack of enthusiasm in the theater was palpable. We encountered the same problem when we invited Sam Peckinpah—our staff refused to interview him. Clint Eastwood had encountered a similar resistance. Today, much more extreme cinematic violence is met with a collective yawn. There was a completely different mind-set in the early 1970s.

Lauren Bacall at the San Francisco International Film Festival. 1973

The sentimental favorite that year was Truman Capote. We showed a short film taken from his story "A Christmas Memory" while Capote sat in the audience, genuinely moved to tears. Shelley Winters was another highlight. She had a reputation for being difficult, and we had a hell of a time finally getting her up there. Shelley always had an excuse. "I can't make it," 'I don't think I want to do it," "I'm not feeling up to it," etc. In 1973, we convinced her to come, but she backed out the week before. "You have to believe me this time," she sniffed over the phone, after crying wolf in years past.

"I really have the flu!" But she finally made it. Once she was on stage, she was terrific. She laughed, cried, and spoke animatedly to the crowd. Our tributes brought out the best in people. Who could resist watching clips of all their best work projected on a large screen to an applauding audience? And by '74, our audience was almost as star-studded as our stage: Jack Nicholson with his date Angelica Huston, Michael Douglas, and Goldie Hawn were a few of the celebrities in the crowd that year.

The festival was running smoothly. The work was mostly seasonal, so I was available to take on another job. Mayor Alioto nominated me to take over as the Managing Director of the War Memorial, the facility that runs the Opera House and the Veterans Building, and later, Davies Symphony Hall. There was some murmuring from the War Memorial Board of Trustees that I ought to have only one city job, but at the mayor's insistence, I took the position and continued as Executive Director of the film festival.

The year 1975 was my tenth year with the festival, and it was more of the same. Our lineup included Joseph Mankiewicz, Gene Hackman, Stanley Donen, Jack Lemmon, Michael Caine, Jane Fonda, and a young Steven Spielberg, who was riding the crest of his first big success, *Jaws*. He was such a new talent that his publicists called and asked if he could come to the festival.

Jane Fonda was making headlines wherever she went in those days. She bailed armed Black Panthers out of jail, got arrested at the airport for assaulting a police officer, and drew heavy criticism for sympathizing with the North Vietnamese, an unpopular stance that earned her the nickname Hanoi Jane. She loved to mix it up and push people's buttons. At one point during her tribute, a reporter took her to task about her political views, and a shouting match ensued. This was San Francisco, so she had a very sympathetic audience. A man in the crowd piped up with, "Leave her alone!"

"Don't defend me," she shot back. "I can stand up for myself." She was not about to have her honor defended by a gentleman. Jane could take it just as well as she could dish it out. It was a very lively afternoon.

At the end of the 1975 event, my two jobs became a public controversy. My ex-colleague Albert Johnson led a charge that I was doing something unlawful or unethical by holding down two city jobs. Before I knew it, I was facing a firestorm of criticism from Albert and his associates. I was accused of "moonlighting" and collecting double paychecks totaling $50,000 yearly and of doing a poor job running the festival. But their allegations were baseless.

Everyone at the War Memorial agreed with Mayor Alioto that there was no conflict of interest as long as I didn't book the film festival at the opera house. As for their claims that the festival was suffering at my hand, the big names we attracted and the sold-out screenings proved them wrong. There had always been egos and temperaments to deal with among the film scholars and board members. This smear campaign struck me as simply a case of sour grapes. It seemed that Albert was hoping I would resign from the festival so he could return and take over.

Articles began appearing in the *San Francisco Chronicle* and *Variety* with my picture next to some ridiculous insinuation. "Is Francis Ford Coppola stage-managing a bloodless coup to overthrow Claude Jarman?" one newspaper asked. Coppola had ties to some people who used to be on the festival board, and the director somehow got unwittingly roped into the campaign against me. In reality, Coppola had no interest in the festival goings-on; he was halfway across the world scouting locations for his passion project *Apocalypse Now*. His associate producer, Mona Skager, issued a statement in my defense, saying, "Francis thinks Jarman has done a dynamite job." Most of the press was sympathetic to my plight, but the divide ran deep. The Bay Area film community, and even Hollywood, was expected to take sides.

I made a trip to Los Angeles during that time and paid a visit to Robert Altman, a director I knew and liked. Altman, bemused, showed me a postcard he had received from San Francisco. On the back was scrawled "Stay out of our city!" It was signed "Mark Chase," one of my associates at the festival. Mark did not send the postcard—it was someone trying to stir up animosity. Thankfully, Robert was a genuine guy with a good sense of humor, and we both laughed it off.

Eventually, the flurry of bad publicity and the pressure of holding both jobs wore on my nerves. The War Memorial trustees were composed of eleven members, and two of them voted to fire me in a board meeting. Weary of the constant conflict, I resigned from the War Memorial, which threw my detractors for a loop. I think Albert expected me to resign from the film festival instead. But the San Francisco International Film Festival was more important to me. With the help of many dedicated allies, I had taken the tiny festival under my wing and nurtured it until it flourished. I couldn't just walk away from it. Not yet.

CHAPTER 11

Moving Forward and Looking Back

The 1970s was the busiest decade of my life. Between running the film festival and serving as Managing Director of the War Memorial complex, I managed to have two more children and produce a feature documentary film. My daughter Natalie was born in 1971, followed by Vanessa in 1972. In fact, Vanessa arrived on the same day that our documentary *Fillmore* opened.

In my off-time from the festival, I had joined Medion, a film production company started by two documentary-filmmaker friends of mine, Dick Heffron and Bert Decker. As part of Guggenheim Productions, they had made political films in the East before moving to the Bay Area. We were planning to produce another political film, but something more exciting presented itself.

In 1971, music promoter Bill Graham announced that he was shutting down the San Francisco rock palace he had made famous, the landmark Fillmore West auditorium. The Grateful Dead, Jefferson Airplane, Santana, and Janis Joplin had all gotten their start on the Fillmore stage. Graham was an intimidating figure, a ruthless negotiator who booked some of the greatest rock acts of the era. Jimi Hendrix, Cream, The Who, Otis Redding, Muddy Waters, Led Zeppelin, The Kinks, The Byrds, The Doors, Credence Clearwater

Revival, Aretha Franklin, Tina Turner, and Pink Floyd were among the Fillmore's headliners. The bands—and the florid psychedelic posters that advertised their concerts—are now legend. Bill Graham was the man behind it all.

When we caught wind that Bill, frustrated over dealing with demanding rock stars, was planning to host one final week of concerts before closing the Fillmore doors for good, we envisioned a documentary. Santana, the Grateful Dead, and Jefferson Airplane would be the main attractions, with Boz Skaggs, Hot Tuna, Quicksilver Messenger Service, and others following on the bill. Bert and Dick went to Bill's staff with a simple request: "We want to film it all."

They readily agreed, though we would still have to obtain permission from each of the bands.

We rounded up a skeleton crew, loaded up a few 16mm cameras, and started shooting.

Getting the bands to agree to appear in the film was our biggest problem. We filmed Bill during the day and the performances at night and spent our spare time haggling with the artists and their managers to secure rights. The Grateful Dead in particular seemed to revel in being uncooperative. They were so anti-establishment, they naturally said no to everything they saw as commercialism or "selling out." It was no secret that they were also using massive amounts of drugs, which complicated the dealings. We asked Bill, "How can we get these guys on board?" He replied, "Buy them a new nose," the implication being that they had destroyed theirs with cocaine.

Bill adored Jerry Garcia and the guys in the Dead but was also exasperated with them, referring to them as "a different species." The feeling was probably mutual. Graham shared a love-hate relationship with most of his favorite groups, which was fascinating to observe. The Fillmore scene was like a close-knit but highly dysfunctional family, and Bill Graham was the scariest father figure imaginable. He was such a vivid character that his antics took center stage in our documentary. This man had fled Nazi Germany as a kid, ending up in a Bronx orphanage with no memory of the first ten years of his life. He was one tough cookie.

By the time the Fillmore closed, we had a few weeks' worth of footage—live performances from the bands, great shots of the audience and of the San Francisco music scene, and hours of Bill losing his temper and shouting obscenities into the telephone. It took us months to narrow the footage down to a focused, feature-length film.

It took even longer to get the Grateful Dead's approval. Without the legal rights to use their performance, there would be no film. We decided to offer to screen them the edited footage of their show, so they could see how they would appear in the movie. The band agreed to watch the clips, on one condition. They insisted that our production company rent a school bus and take them to a drive-in movie first. So after busing the Grateful Dead to a drive-in, wining and dining them with popcorn and hot dogs, we screened the footage and finally got their signature on the dotted line. Unfortunately, the delay meant that by the time we had the rights, the Fillmore had been closed for nearly a year and was old news.

We rushed to get the film done but were further delayed when we ran out of funds. I put in a call to my mentor Clarence Brown. "We need $100,000 to finish the film," I said, and he replied, "Okay," just like that. Once again, Clarence's unwavering belief in me saved the day.

Once the film was edited, a distribution deal was our next hurdle. We suspected there was a market for *Fillmore* because *Woodstock* had been a big hit for Warner Bros. the year before. But navigating the new Hollywood was a challenge. I had no connections in that world. After a few dead-end leads and unreturned phone calls, the head of Twentieth Century Fox, Gordon Stulberg, showed up in our office and offered to buy the film. The day was saved once again.

Fox did a credible job distributing *Fillmore,* and it was fairly successful. Dick, Bert, and I were a little crestfallen that it didn't receive more attention, but by the time it was finally released, the Fillmore West music scene was long gone. Also, Bill Graham was not the most beloved man in town. Many people stayed away from the film because they saw Bill as a bully.

And he was. But he was also a trained actor, and a great deal of his bullying was theatrical. He sure knew how to put on a show.

Later, when it came time to repay Clarence, I went down to Los Angeles and screened the finished product for him. I was a little nervous, since Bill Graham expressed everything in four-letter words. It was like watching an R-rated movie with your dad. I was cringing. In the first five minutes of the film, Bill kicks a musician out of his office, warning the poor guy, "Next time you say 'fuck you' to me, I'll take your teeth out of your mouth and shove 'em up your nose!" *Fillmore* is filled with such scenes. But Clarence was an artist, and he saw the film's merit. He said nothing about the profanity, just "I'm pleased that I was able to help." I handed him a check and said, "Here's your money back, thank you very much." That was it.

The next project we planned for Medion was a film adaptation of Tom McGuane's outrageous novel *The Bushwhacked Piano*. We got McGuane himself to write the script and hoped to cast Ryan O'Neal in the lead. Ryan was interested but was dating Barbra Streisand at the time, who apparently disapproved of the project. Without Ryan on board, we had no star power and no funding. Dick Heffron spotted an intense young actor who we thought would be great in the lead. His name was Robert De Niro, and he had a small role in a mafia comedy called *The Gang That Couldn't Shoot Straight.* One meeting with De Niro convinced us he was witty and a risk-taker. We knew he could perfectly embody Nicholas Payne, McGuane's oddball hero. But the name De Niro meant nothing in the industry in 1971. Robert De Niro was just a year or two away from a star-making partnership with Martin Scorsese, but at the time, he was too obscure to get our movie funded. We never made *The Bushwhacked Piano* and soon disbanded our production company.

At least we got one small but culturally significant film made. I introduced Dick Heffron to my old *Hangman's Knot* director, Roy Huggins, and he went on to a successful television career. Bill Graham turned his attention to organizing and promoting large-scale concerts, including Live Aid in 1985. I was shocked when Bill was killed in a helicopter crash in 1991. *Fillmore* not only captured the last days of the San Francisco hippie-rock era but captured the incomparable Bill Graham at his worst and his best. I'm so glad the film exists.

The city of San Francisco had weathered the storms of the Vietnam War—the protests, the anger, the disillusionment—and so had the SFIFF. The year 1976 was the festival's twentieth anniversary, and we went all out. Black-tie celebrations, special A-list guests, and a retrospective of our greatest films made it a memorable year. Jack Nicholson, who had just taken home a Best Actor Oscar for *One Flew Over the Cuckoo's Nest*, was the guest of honor. He brought along his friend (and producer of *Chinatown*) Robert Evans for an entertaining day of clips, questions, and answers.

Our opening-night emcee was Merv Griffin. Merv had a background in music and was known to play a little piano and sing now and then. When I heard that Tony Bennett was in town performing at the Fairmont, I called Merv and arranged a surprise to kick off the festival in style. In front of a packed house, Merv walked on stage and sat down at the piano. "I was born in the Bay Area, in San Mateo," he said, "and it's always been my dream to sing this song." He started singing the opening verse of the classic, "I left my heart . . ."

Behind him, the curtains parted and out stepped Tony Bennett himself to finish the verse, ". . . in San Francisco." The crowd went wild, and Tony completed the song as only he could.

Burt Lancaster was on hand for a tribute, along with the lady I had met in that RKO classroom thirty years earlier, Natalie Wood. She was overwhelmed by the outpouring of love and respect when the audience saw her entire career pieced together starting with her first film at age six. Natalie had never seen her twenty-five-year screen evolution in one sitting. Her voice was a little shaky and her eyes a little misty when she said, "What an incredible experience to see your life flash before your eyes!"

Our new mayor was George Moscone, a man I knew to be a true film buff. I arranged a lunch at the North Beach restaurant for Mayor Moscone, Natalie Wood, her husband Robert Wagner, myself, and Gary Shansby, one of the festival board members. We had a wonderful time. I have often reflected on that lunch. Just two years later, George Moscone, along with Supervisor Harvey Milk, were assassinated at City Hall by a crazed former supervisor. A few years after that, Natalie also died a sudden, tragic death. That afternoon when we sat and ate Italian food was the last time I saw her.

The 1978 festival was dominated by European films and filmmakers. We had Claude Chabrol in person to discuss his latest project "Violette," along with selections from Yugoslavia and Czechoslovakia, and everyone's favorite French actor Yves Montand. We planned to devote an evening to Luis Bunuel, the surrealist master behind *Belle de Jour* and *That Obscure Object of Desire,* but Bunuel was badly hurt in an accident and had to cancel. We recovered from our disappointment with a Paul Mazursky tribute, which was a crowd-pleaser.

I had already decided that the 1979 festival would be my last. Fifteen years was enough. With the exception of Welles and Bunuel, we had been able to wrangle just about all the major actors and directors to San Francisco to be feted. We had imported an incredible array of foreign films that would otherwise never have been seen by American audiences. In short, I had seen and done it all. It was time to move on.

There was one actor who had never been to the festival, and he was one of my all-time favorites: Sir Alec Guinness. For years, Guinness had politely declined our invitations. This man had been awarded an Oscar, a BAFTA, and a Golden Globe for *The Bridge on the River Kwai* and had played a record nine different characters in *Kind Hearts and Coronets.* I admired his talent and grace. With the arguable exception of Laurence Olivier, he was the ultimate living actor. For my final year, I was determined to pay tribute to Sir Alec.

I went to London that spring and called his agent directly. When he told me, "I will pass your request on to Mr. Guinness," in his clipped British accent, I feared another polite rejection. Imagine my surprise when, an hour later, Sir Alec himself returned my call. He couldn't have been nicer. "Let's get together," he suggested. Over lunch, he told me he'd be delighted to attend the festival. I was elated and pleased to discover that he was a wonderful man—very friendly, honest, and true to his word. When he stepped off the plane in San Francisco, he told me he'd been down with the flu for five days. "You almost lost me," he said. But he was determined to recover in time to keep his promise.

In my last board meeting, I recommended that Albert Johnson be invited to return to the festival. He had been an integral part of the event. I knew he missed working with us, and we missed him and his vast knowledge of film. It felt good to bury the hatchet. Albert and I worked together one last time as he created a beautiful tribute to Sir Alec Guinness, weaving together his greatest movie moments, starting with *Great Expectations* in 1946 and ending with his iconic portrayal of Obi-Wan Kenobi in *Star Wars* in 1977. This tribute was so special that, for the first time ever, we scheduled it instead of a film screening for opening night. It was a sold-out smash at $125 per ticket, and we repeated the program the following afternoon for the public, who paid the $1 admission.

Accompanied by his wife, Merula, Alec was the soul of courtesy and seemed sincerely touched by the appreciative audience. A lovely time was had by all. Before he boarded the plane back to England, I threw a party for Alec at my house. When George Lucas found out, he made sure he was also invited. Lucas wanted a chance to sweet-talk Guinness into making an appearance in the *Star Wars* sequel he was planning, *The Empire Strikes Back*. Apparently their chat went well because Alec agreed to make a cameo. I don't think Alec was particularly proud of being known as Obi-Wan Kenobi, but he acknowledged that the franchise gave his career and his finances a big boost.

I left the festival on a high note. In fifteen years, we had made San Francisco the premiere film-festival destination of the West Coast, if not the entire United States. With our appreciation for classic Hollywood, we exposed audiences to the craftsmanship of filmmakers like Hawks, Ford, and Capra, laying the groundwork for Ted Turner's Turner Classic Movies and the classic film preservation movement led by Martin Scorsese in the 1990s.

By the time the 1980s rolled around, dozens of film festivals had cropped up in Los Angeles, Chicago, and many smaller cities. I was gratified to see the idea spread like wildfire. Today, most major cities host some type of annual film festival, and ours was the first in the country. We were the pioneers.

In 1978, Mayor Moscone called me and said that one of the trustees who had voted to fire me from the War Memorial board was up for reappointment. "How would you like to take his place?" he asked. I jumped at the opportunity to replace the man who had made my life difficult. Shortly after our conversation, Mayor Moscone was assassinated, and his successor, Mayor Diane Feinstein followed through with my appointment. I ended up serving on the War Memorial board for thirty-five years.

I even gave TV acting one more chance and took a final turn in front of the cameras. Like half of Hollywood and some of the UK, I appeared in *Centennial,* the Western miniseries based on the writings of James Michener. The all-star cast included Richard Chamberlain, Timothy Dalton, Lynn Redgrave, and Andy Griffith. It was my first acting job in twenty years.

John Wilder, producer of the TV series *The Streets of San Francisco,* had become a good friend of mine. As the producer of *Centennial,* he offered me a meaty role as a farmer named Earl Grebe, and since the festival had ended, I accepted. For my scenes, I spent six weeks in Greeley, Colorado, in ten-degree weather. It was quite a switch from California, and I loved it. When the cameras rolled, I felt right at home. I even entertained thoughts about resurrecting my film career and doing more work. But about one week before wrapping up the series, I noticed the actors getting nervous and calling their agents. There was a hint of panic in their voices when they asked, "What have you got lined up next for me?" They had no idea when they would work again, or where their next job was coming from. What would they do now? I, on the other hand, knew exactly what I was going to do. I was going home to my stable life. I never pursued acting again.

I started my own company, hoping to escape the constant massaging of delicate egos found in the film community. I opened an elite travel agency where my old Hollywood training served me well once again—I booked entertainment and guest speakers like Neil Armstrong and Tennessee Ernie Ford for business executives traveling to London, Paris, Tahiti, you name it. I enjoyed the work, but I learned that inflated egos populate every industry. They are inescapable.

In 1983, Maryann and I were divorced. Like Clarence Brown, it took me a few tries to get it right, but in 1986, I married Katie Stuart. Our twin daughters, Charlotte and Sarah, came along in 1994 to round out the family. To go along with my seven children, I now have eight grandchildren. My sister Mildred married a widower with three children and moved to Atlanta to raise her family. Katie and I moved to Marin County, north of San Francisco.

When the insurance company transferred me to the Bay Area in 1961, I had no idea I would spend the rest of my life there. But I fell in love with the city of San Francisco, the Northern California coast, and the surrounding areas. I've lived in California for sixty years, but when people ask where I'm from, I always reply, "Nashville." I'm still the kid in the Nashville classroom who got discovered one day. My life took a detour into the world of the movies, and I never quite recovered.

In 1998 and again in 2003, every living Academy Award winner was brought to the Oscars ceremony and introduced. It was an Oscar family reunion. We sat alphabetically, and once again, I was seated near Jennifer Jones, recalling the anniversary luncheon at MGM all those years ago. After the 2003 broadcast, I received a letter from my old *Roughshod* costar, Myrna Dell. She said how happy she was to see me again. "Looking at you now," she wrote, "all I can say is, back then you were too young for me, and now you're too old!"

Robert De Niro was there too. We hadn't spoken in years, but he spotted me backstage and must have remembered our 1971 meeting. He came up to me and said, "You look familiar. I've met you somewhere before."

"We had coffee thirty years ago," I reminded him. We both laughed and reminisced about *The Bushwhacked Piano,* the film that never got made.

In the age we live in now, the art of filmmaking has been replaced by big-budget corporate franchises that generate merchandise. Movie-related tie-ins like T-shirts and videogames earn more revenue than the movies themselves. Occasionally, great films are still made. The difference is, they are usually made outside of the current Hollywood system, whereas in the past, the system was estab-

lished for the purpose of making great films. It didn't always succeed, but producing high-quality entertainment was the rule, not
the exception. Despite all of our technological progress, nothing in
Hollywood today compares to the studio-era pioneers, those men
and women with the vision and the skill to create lasting entertainment. The Clarence Browns, John Fords, and Louis B. Mayers are
gone; they belong to another era.

But I'm still here. I've seen the postwar glory of the studio system, the decline of Hollywood at the hands of television, the 1960s
wave of foreign and experimental films, the Reagan era (who'd have
dreamed one of my old Hollywood acquaintances would be president?), the death of celluloid film, and the rise of the digital age. I
went from watching movies in the front row of the Belmont Theater
every weekend, to acting in them in Hollywood, to celebrating them
in San Francisco, to producing them, and back to watching them
again. I'm retired now and have been to screenings all over the country discussing my films. I'm filled with pride to see *The Yearling,
Rio Grande,* and *Intruder in the Dust* projected to new audiences.
I avoided watching my movies for years. It took me a long time to
enjoy seeing that blond kid up there on the screen. Now, I think he's
not so bad.

The films themselves will never grow old because they were
made with such care. I didn't fully appreciate the studio system when
I was dropped into it at age ten. Now I know we will never see the
likes of Hollywood's Golden Age again. That level of quality is gone
with the wind. It is an era worthy of remembrance.

The Academy Awards with Katie Jarman
and Julie Andrews. 1998

Academy Awards Acting Award Winners. 2003

I went to school on the MGM lot with Margaret
O'Brien, Jane Powell, and Elizabeth Taylor.

Jane Wyman and Gregory Peck were my parents in *"The Yearling"*.

With my father in Oxford, Mississippi, where we
filmed *"Intruder in the Dust"* (1949)

My introduction at the 2003 Academy Awards show

ACKNOWLEDGMENTS

In 2008, my wife Katie surprised me, my family and many friends with a film she had produced and directed which basically told my life story. It was shown on the big screen in our local movie theater. Seeing the film inspired me to follow her suggestion to write a book about my life in Hollywood during the "golden era" that no longer exists. About eighteen months ago I decided to move ahead with that goal. My thanks to my daughter Natalie Jarman who works in the entertainment business in Hollywood and introduced me to two of her friends, Jeffrey Vance, a writer/producer and Sloan de Forest, a freelance writer. Jeffrey was a helpful advisor and strategist. Sloan, an incredible talent, was the person who helped me write my story and I am very grateful for her invaluable assistance with this book. I also want to thank my daughter Vanessa Getty who has helped me maneuver though the literary world to get my work in print.

ABOUT THE AUTHOR

Discovered by legendary MGM director Clarence Brown in 1945 in a fifth-grade classroom in Nashville, Tennessee, at the age of ten, Jarman was whisked away to the movie capital of the world where he would star with Gregory Peck and Jane Wyman in the film *The Yearling*, based on a Pulitzer Prize–winning book written by Marjorie Kinnan Rawlings. He received an Academy Award for his performance. He remained at MGM for five years before the advent of television signaled the end of the old Hollywood and its star system. Jarman went on to make ten additional films, including playing the son of John Wayne and Maureen O'Hara in John Ford's epic western *Rio Grande* and the film noir classic *Intruder in the Dust*, William Faulkner's story of a lynching in the South. Jarman lives in Marin County north of San Francisco with his wife, Katie, and their twin daughters, Charlotte and Sarah. He has five children from his two previous marriages: Claude Jarman III, Murray Jarman, Elizabeth Suddeth, Natalie Jarman and Vanessa Getty. This is his first book.

CPSIA information can be obtained
at www.ICGtesting.com
Printed in the USA
LVHW012006020320
648718LV00006B/716

9 781640 036673